New
MOUNTA ⟨√ **W9-DED-665**

I dedicate this book about Mountain folks to my wife, Sandra Howard Cahill, whose roots are in Keene and Wilmot-Flat, New Hampshire. After 25 years of marriage I have discovered that you can take the girl out of the mountains, but you can't take the mountains out of the girl.

Bob Cahill

Indian chief Chocorua is about to leap from his ledge as New Hampshire's Cornelius Campbell prepares to shoot him—from a painting by Thomas Cole.

Cover Photos: ISBN 0-916787-14-1

Monument to the Indians, "Hail To The Sunrise," Mohawk Trail, Massachusetts. The Madison Spring Hut of New Hampshire's Presidential Range, built in 1888, photo taken in 1890. Profile of New Hampshire's Old Man of the Mountain. A snowshoe treck up the mountain at Jackson, New Hampshire, photos taken in 1906. The haunted Hoosac Tunnel. (Photos courtesy of the Appalachian Mountain Club, Boston, MA.)

Introduction

My wife's family, the Howards, own a tiny tar-roofed "cabin" in the woods, half way up the side of New Hampshire's Mount Kearsarge. In an effort to confuse visitors, especially those from Massachusetts, New Hampshire folks have named two of their mountains "Kearsarge." One is near North Conway and is also known by its old Indian name, "Pequaket;" the other rises majestically above Wilmot-Flat. And if you don't know where Wilmot-Flat is, it's right next to Potter Place, only four miles from Cilleyville. It is this second Mount Kearsarge where the Howard "cabin" is located. The mountain is sparsely settled with Howards or those who are related in some way to Howards.

The "cabin," which my wife and children prefer to call "camp," was built some fifty years ago by her father. He also built the little house with the seat in it that stands near the "camp." Both leave much to be desired. I am not one that needs all the comforts and conveniences of life to be content, but I do enjoy an occasional bath or shower. At "camp," one must either wait for a rainstorm or drive some five miles down the winding mountain road to Pleasant Lake, where soap must not be used for it will kill the fish. At night, when blackness sets in, other animals can be heard scratching around the outhouse, so when nature calls, one must wait until the sun comes up and the little animals, whatever they are, are gone, or at least silent. Exciting evening activities might be listening to the hoot of an owl or the rustle of birches wavering in the wind. One could, of course, wander down to the base of the mountain to Wilmot-Flat, where the main event of the month is the church bean-supper, featuring soloist Mary Grace Howard singing, "Let's All Gather By The River," accompanied by Sarah May Howard on the piano.

Camp is full of wood-mice, which visibly scatter in every direction when the door is opened. They live in bureau drawers, in beds and in the furniture, but my wife and children never seem to mind this. Yet, at home in Salem, Massachusetts, if a mouse is ever spotted in the house, screams of terror echo through the neighborhood. And it's not just mice and other little animals that roam the woods around the camp, hunters shot a bear only a few yards from the outhouse a few years ago. This didn't seem to bother my wife and kids one bit, but it petrified me.

For the safety of my family, I sacrificed my prejudices against mountain living, and now join them on every trip to camp. It was during one of these recent reluctant sojourns that I began to relax and enjoy the peaceful surroundings and to realize that there is a magic here in the hills that cannot be found in the lowlands... and there are mind-bogling mysteries here as well. This book is about them.

I
Old Indian Myths

According to the dictionary, a myth is *"a fable, a legend embodying primitive faith in the supernatural."* Indian historian William Simmons in his book *"Spirit of the New England Tribes"*, writes *"myths are actual accounts of early happenings—often sacred truths of Indian culture..."*

There are many old Indian myths and legends in New England; some of them based on superstitions and primitive fears, but a few of these stories passed on from generation to generation through oral traditions are based on fact. John Josselyn, in his book, *"Two Voyages To New England,"* published in 1680, writes *"No Indian will set foot on the mountain Agiocochook* [Mount Washington], *as it is the Shrine of the Great Spirit. Ask the Indian whither he goes when he dies, he will tell you, pointing with his finger to heaven, beyond the White Mountains, and hint at the great flood, as may be conceived by a story they have received from father to son, that a great while ago their country drowned, and all people and other creatures in it. Only one Powaw and his wife, forseeing the flood, fled to the White Mountains carrying a hare along with them and so escaped. After a while the Powaw sent the hare away, who, not returning emboldened thereby they descended, and lived many years after, and had many children, from whom the Country was filled again with Indians."*

This old New England Indian legend sounds like the biblical Noah's Ark story, yet, if it is not based on ancient fact, where and how on earth did the story originate? Could the Indians have made it up? The story of Noah could have been told to them by some early explorer or missionary and then changed a bit to suit their own purposes. But that does seem rather doubtful.

"In the mythology of the savage," noted Salem author Nathanial Hawthorne tells us, *"these mountains were considered sacred and inaccessible, full of unearthly wonders, illuminated at lofty heights by the blaze of the precious stones, and inhabited by deities, who sometimes shrouded themselves in the snowstorm and came down on the lower world."* All New England tribes believed that climbing the highest mountain, Agiocochook, meant meeting the Great Spirit face to face, and certain death to any bold brave who attempted the climb. June of 1642, Darby Field, a daring Irishman and a recent resident of Exeter, New Hampshire, decided to climb Mount Agiocochook. The Indians living in the Pascataquack region nearest to the mountain, were surprised and upset with Darby, for they feared he would enrage the Great Spirit. This was the first known mountain climbing expedi-

tion in America. Although a few courageous Indians agreed to accompany Darby to the mountain and even up the slopes for a short distance, only two of them would go to the top of the mountain with him. Governor Winthop of the Mass Bay Colony writes about Darby's exploits in his Journal—June, 1642:

"One Darby Field, an Irishman, living about Pascataquack, being accompanied with two Indians, went to the top of the white hill. He made his journey in 18 days. It was about one hundred miles from Saco, that after forty miles travel he did, for the most part, ascend, and within ten miles of the top was neither tree nor grass. Some of them (the Indians) accompanied him within eight miles of the top, but durst go no further, telling him that no Indian ever dared go higher, and that he would die if he went. So they staid there till his return, but his two Indians took courage by his example and went with him.

They went divers times through the thick clouds for a good space, and within four miles of the top they had no clouds, but very cold... On the north side there was such a precipece, as they could scarcely discern to the bottom. They had neither cloud nor wind at the top, and moderate heat. All the country about him seemed a level, except here and there a hill rising above the rest, but far beneath them.... He found there much Mucovy glass (mica), they could rive out pieces of forty feet long and seven or eight broad. When he came back to the Indians, he found them drying themselves by the fire, for they had had a great tempest of wind and rain...."

Of the Indians who courageously joined Darby's expedition, noted 18th century historian Samuel Adams Drake tells us, *"several of the Pigwacket Tribe, rendered foolhardy by their successor of exorcising evil spirits, so far conquered their fears as to ascend the mountain; but they never returned, and had, no doubt, expiated their folly by being transformed into stone, or flung headlong down some stark and terrible precipece."*

Darby Field reported that the mountain was strewn with *"shining-stones"* thought to be diamonds. Even prior to Darby's climb, Englishman Christopher Levett, exploring the coast of Maine in 1623, reported: *"the savages here say this River (the Saco) commeth from a great mountain called Christal Hill, being as they say one hundred miles in the Country, yet it is to be seen at the sea side."* So, the Indians called the mountains of Maine and New Hampshire the *"Crystal Hills,"* even before Darby announced to the world that he had found crystals, or *"shining stones"* on top of Agiocochook.

Within a few weeks, July 1642, Darby Field led another expedition to the top of New England's highest mountain. This time he had five other White Men with him. These were not sportsmen or adventurers, but fortune seekers, interested only in the precious gems that the mountain might relinquish to them. *"They had some wind at the top of the mountain,"* writes Governor Winthop in his Journal, concerning this second climb to the summit, *"and some clouds,"* he adds, *"which hid the sun. They brought some stones which they supposed had been diamonds, but they were most crystal."* And worthless!

There was, however, a giant valuable gem, deep red in color, to be found in the mountains, the Indians assured the first white settlers. It was of immense size, hanging high up on the side of one of the White Mountains, overlooking a large pond. Indians who confessed to the whites that they had seen this marvelous stone, were either sworn to secrecy by their chiefs concerning its location, or they were so hypnotized by its beauty that they could not recall the location. Indian legend was that the tribal chiefs who had seen the jewel were obsessed by it and wanted to have it for their own. They dared not remove it from its perch, however, because it belonged to the Great Spirit. Some chiefs had gone back to behold its beauty and luster many times. Even white hunters and explorers of the mountain wilderness said they had seen the jewel shining from its high perch miles away in the forests at night, but it was deep in the mountains and could not be found when they searched for it in daylight.

"If a White Man came to steal the Great Gem," the Indians warned, *"a mist from the magic pond would hide the gem from him."* This myth was believed by many New Englanders, well into the 18th century. Jeremy Belknap, in his *"History of New Hampshire,"* writes that, *"From the Indians and from the captives whom they sometimes led to Canada through the passes of these mountains, many fictions have been propogated, which have given rise to marvelous and incredible stories; particularly, it has been reported, that at immense and inaccessible heights, there have been carbuncles, which are suppose to appear luminous in the night."* John Sullivan, in his *"History of Maine,"* wrote that, *"Even well after the American Revolutionary War, many still believed in the existence of the Great Carbuncle."*

"The Great Carbuncle," was the title of one of Nat Hawthorne's short stories in his book, *"Twice Told Tales."* In this story, the main character is a man who, *"was one of those ill-fated mortals, such as the Indians told of, whom, in their early youth, the Great Carbuncle smote with a peculiar madness.... All who visited that region, knew him as the seeker, and by no other name. As no one could remember when he first took up the search, there went a fable in the Valley of the Saco that for his inordinate lust after*

the Great Carbuncle, he had been condemned to wander among the mountains till the end of time, still with the same feverish hopes at sunrise, the same despair at eve. " The old Indian tradition, wrote Hawthorne, was that *"a spirit kept watch about the gem, and bewildered those who sought it, either by removing it from its peak, to peak of the higher hills, or by calling up a mist from the enchanted lake over which it hung."*

The Indians insisted that hunting parties *"a full forty miles south of the White Mountains, awoke at midnight and beheld the Great Carbuncle gleaming like a meteor, so that the shadows of the trees fell backward from it.... A light that overpowered the moon and almost matched the sun."* The Indians declared that no mortal hand could ever touch the *"great firestone,"* as Samuel Adams Drake called it. Those who actually spent precious time searching for it without success began to wonder if the radiant gem might have loosened from the high ledge and fallen into the depths of the pond below.

The Great Carbuncle myth and its illusive setting does, however, closely resemble the natural perfection and lofty site of a real stone wonder in the New Hampshire mountains, which wasn't discovered by White Men until the year 1805. Two workmen repairing the mountain road at Franconia Notch were bathing in Echo Lake after a long hard day of labor. Looking up, they were amazed at what they saw hanging from a steep mountain cliff high above their heads. It was a giant brooding face of granite, staring out over the lake. The workmen thought the great stone face looked like Thomas Jefferson, but once they announced their discovery, many others came to admire this strange quirk of nature. Most thought the face resembled that of an Indian, so the projecting human-like rock formation was called, *"Indian Head."* Today, it is also known as *"The Profile, The Old Stone Face,"* and *"The Old Man Of The Mountain."* The grim face hangs some 1,200 feet above Echo Lake from the steep side of Cannon Mountain. It measures ninety feet from forehead to jutting jaw, twenty feet from cheekbone to cheekbone, and has a rocky nose that's forty feet long. Legend is that Indians knew it was there all along and that their forefathers worshipped the great stone face. It is said that Chief Pemigewasset used the stone face to spy on his enemies, who often attempted to sneak into his tribal territories from Canada. In those days, according to the Indians, the Great Stone Face could speak, but he shut his granite trap when the White Men arrived on the scene.

It was the White Men who actually sealed the Old Man's mouth shut, when it was discovered his jaw was slipping. Although the profile looks like one enormous sad face, it is actually made up of three separate massive rock ledges, which had to undergo a facelift because the ledge that makes up the chin was falling. It is now anchored in place with chains. One wonders if the Great Stone Face, lodged into the side of a mountain and directly over a body of water, like the legendary Great Carbuncle, may have given rise to the carbuncle legend. Maybe the Indian Head had a radiant jewel imbedded in its forehead, like the Moonstone of India, and an earthquake loosened the giant jewel causing it to drop into Echo Lake.

Some Indians referred to the territory in and around Franconia Notch, as *"a place of demons,"* yet it was also considered holy ground by many Indians. Old Doc Willey, a New Hampshire historian and humorist, considered all of New Hampshire holy ground. He once said, *"Men put out signs representing their different trades; jewelers hung out a monster watch, shoemakers, a large boot, and up in Franconia, God Almighty has hung out a sign that, in New England, He makes men!"*

Less than two miles north of The Old Man Of The Mountain, is an overgrown ghost town, which in the late 1850s, was an active village of some fifty homes, two churches, a general store, blacksmith shop and schoolhouse. The adult male villagers worked a newly opened copper mine there, and the railroad ran up that way. It had the makings of an up-and-coming prosperous community. But Indians living up that way today will tell you that everyone living there then, men, women, children, and even cats and dogs, disappeared in a day and a night in August of 1859. They were never seen again, and only because they didn't heed the warnings of Indians who had come down from Canada to insist that they move their village. The reason that these Indians wanted them to move their buildings a few hundred yards from where they stood, is that the village was built on an ancient Indian burial ground. It was holy land. The copper mine owners, who ignored the Indians pleas, were continuously warned that the Great Spirit would seek revenge on the mine workers and their families if the village wasn't moved. After their many requests fell on deaf ears, the Canadian Indians, whose ancestors were buried beneath the village, left the Franconia area, and the white settlers breathed a sigh of relief. A few days after their departure, *"there came a great thunder,"* say the few remaining New Hampshire Indians, *"and the sky over the village turned to blood."* Even White Men who were traveling the notch that day, said that the sky took on *"a copper-hue, and the ground trembled."* It was reported that sixty-one miners were crushed in a massive mine cave-in, and that some women and children suffocated from an explosion of copper-dust. Three days later, there wasn't a person or domestic animal to be found at the village, just empty houses. The mine owners wanted to reopen the mine, but no one would work or live there, some say, because of the death of all the menfolk. But others say that the workers and their families were spirited away by the Indian curse on the land. Today, just old cellar holes, decaying buildings, tall grass and weeds cover those sloping mounds of earth. And, under the mounds lie the ancient natives of this land. May they rest in peace!

There is another cursed village in the New Hampshire mountains, embroiled in Indian lore, and like the old copper mine legend, the curse is based on fact. Leaving Cannon Mountain and Franconia Notch, you travel down Route Three, head east on the very scenic Kancamangus Highway, and you come to Conway, New Hampshire, near the Maine border. Here you'll see, lifting to the sky, New England's most popular mountain—Chocorua! John Greeleaf Whittier called Chocorua *"the most beautiful and striking of all the New Hampshire Hills."* It is the most easterly of what is called the Sandwich Range, and is barely 3,500 feet high, but its mountain setting is breathtaking. Reverend Thomas Starr King, New Hampshire's first mountain historian, wrote, *"Certainly, there is to be seen in New England, no other region so swathed in dreamy charm."* It was Darby Field again, while on his way to climb Mount Washington, who was the first White Man to see Mount Chocorua, calling it *"a striking sentinel."* Of the surrounding countryside, he wrote: *"I have found ten falls of the river* [Saco] *and two thousand acres of rich meadow in Peqwagget, an Indian town."* Yet, because of the hostile Indians of Peqwagget, it was over one hundred years after Darby's discovery that the area was settled by White Men. The Massachusetts government, which New Hampshire was then a part, allowed settlement for rent, *"if demanded, of one ear of Indian corn each year for ten years."* The town of Conway was built on the site of the ancient village of Peqwagget, which was abandoned by the Indians in May of 1725, within one day, and their exodus was the stimulus for the legendary *"Curse of Chocorua."*

The Peqwagget Indians had been causing the colonists trouble since 1703, when they joined with the Canadian French against the British in Queen Anne's War. An invading army of British and Colonial troops marched into the mountains to wipe out these Indians, but the expedition got lost in the wilderness, and the Indians escaped destruction. A bounty of forty pounds for the scalp of any Peqwagget Indian was offered by the Massachusetts government, which had some greedy bounty-hunters snowshoeing into the mountains that winter searching for Peqwaggets. Five scalps were turned into the governor at Boston before the snow cleared from the mountain tops. In 1724, the Peqwaggets attacked the village of Dunstable (Nashua, New Hampshire), killing nine men and taking two hostage. The governor then raised the bounty to 100 British pounds for every Peqwaggest Indian scalp delivered to him in Boston. A British Army captain, named Lovewell, organized a 46-man volunteer army, made up mainly of men from Dunstable, and headed up to Peqwagget territory. Lovewell was determined to wipe out the bothersome mountain tribe and, at the same time, make a fine fortune for himself with their scalps. The captain was already a notorious Indian killer, after having led an expedition into what is now Wakefield, New Hampshire. There, he and his men had come upon ten Indians sleeping in the forest. He had his men *"shoot them before they waken,"* and then he had all ten scalped. The bloody head pieces were delivered to the Governor of Massachusetts.

On May 7, 1725, Lovewell and his men reached Peqwagget territory, and camped out on the banks of a small lake, now called Lovewell's Pond, planning to attack the Indian village next day. Instead, a small Indian hunting party, under the leadership of a sachem named Paugus, discovered the invaders and ambushed them, immediately killing eight of the White Men and wounding Captain Lovewell. Lovewell ordered a counter attack and in this second skirmish, Paugus was killed. The fighting went on all day with heavy casualties on both sides. By nightfall, Captain Lovewell died of his wounds, as did Captain Frye, his second in command. Twelve others were dead, with only eight men in Lovewell's little army not suffering from serious wounds. The Indians, under command of a brave named Wahwa, fought for two hours into the night, but then withdrew to Peqwagget Village. On May 13th, eleven men of Lovewell's army staggered into Dunstable, and two crawled into town the following day. The fierce fighting had almost eliminated all participants on both sides. It was the first and last Indian battle in the mountains of New England, known today as *"The Battle Of Lovewell's Pond."* It frightened the Peqwagget tribe enough to make them leave New England for good. They picked up their village, lock, stock and barrel and moved to Saint Francis in Canada, on the banks of the St. Lawrence River. They never returned. Only one Peqwagget Indian opted to remain behind. He was a bold chief named Chocorua.

Chocorua hunted the mountains with his young son Taumba, instilling in the boy that this land was his land, and not the White Man's. The chief did, however, befriend one white settler named Cornelius Campbell, who lived with his wife and ten year old son at what is now Tamworth, New Hampshire. One day Chocorua was called away to a tribal Powow at Saint Francis, Canada. He decided to leave his son with the Campbells for them to care for while he was away. This pleased Taumba who, Chocorua felt, was too young for such an exhausting journey. Taumba loved Caroline Campbell's home cooking and the company of young Cornelius Junior. Living with the Campbells only a few weeks, the curious Taumba, always anxious to try a new and different White Man's food, mistakenly swallowed a poison that Mr. Campbell was preparing to set out for wolves that were attacking his farm cattle. Taumba died, and two days later, Campbell buried the Indian boy on his farm.

Two months later, on a day when Cornelius Campbell was away at market, Chocorua returned. When Caroline Campbell broke the sad news to the Indian Chief, he went wild. He slit Caroline Campbell's throat, then mortally wounded her young son. In a screeching, agonizing rage, he ran off to the mountains. When Cornelius returned to his cabin and found his slain family in the cabin, he knew that Chocorua was to blame. He grabbed his musket and headed for the mountain that was the chief's favorite hunting ground. Campbell pursued Chocorua to the highest peak of that mountain. Knowing that he was about to be shot by the only White Man he had ever befriended, Chocorua lifted his arms to the clouds and shouted: *"Evil spirits breathe death upon the cattle of the White Man. Wind and fire destroy your dwellings. Panthers and wolves howl and fatten on your bones. Chocorua goes now to the Great Spirit."* Before Campbell could fire his musket, Chocorua leaped off the mountain-top, crashing into the rocks far below!

Cornelius Campbell died of unknown causes exactly two years later. When his body was found in the woods near his cabin, he had been partially eaten by wolves. Mountain people believed in Chocorua's curse for many years, and it actually disuaded many potential farmers from settling near Conway, New Hampshire, which once was the home of the Peqwagget tribe. Exactly 100 years after the death of Peqwagget Chief Chocorua, a devastating pestilence killed all the cattle from Albany, New Hampshire to Conway. The New Hampshire farmers were convinced it was Chocorua fulfilling his curse, but experts from Dartmouth College concluded it was mud-lime that was contaminating the water and killing the cows. Even today in the mountains of Conway and North Conway, few scoff at Chocorua's Curse. For, although superstitions and fears are somewhat tempered in our modern day society, New Englanders know that the legends and myths of the mountain Indians are mostly based on fact and truth.

"It is unwise," mountain folks will tell you, *"not to heed the advise or warnings of Indians, for their ancestors have left them with a magical power that cannot be equalled nor understood by the White Man"*—Tread softly on his old hunting grounds, and not at all on his old burying grounds.

II
House Of The Willeys

"It was now the middle of September. We had come since sunrise from Bartlett, passing up through the valley of the Saco, which extends between mountainous walls, sometimes with a steep ascent, but often as level as a church aisle... We had mountains behind us and mountains on each side, and a group of mightier ones ahead... It is, indeed, a wondrous path... This is the Notch of the White Hills. We had now reached a narrow passage, which showed almost the appearance of having been cut by human strength and artifice in the solid rock. There was a wall of granite on each side, high and precipitous, especially on our right, and so smooth that a few evergreens could hardly find foothold enough to grow there. This is the entrance of the romantic defile of the Notch...passing through a deep pine forest, which for some miles allowed us to see nothing but its own dismal shade...."

And this is the impression that my fellow Salemite, Nat Hawthorne, had during his first visit to Crawford Notch in New Hampshire's White Mountains in 1832. The air in this dark passage through the mountains, *"was now sharp and cold,"* wrote Hawthorne in his *"Sketches From Memory,"* like that of *"a clear November evening."* The steep surrounding mountains that hemmed in this wondrous path, he called *"majestic, and even awful."* There was an unpleasantness about Crawford Notch, and that was what attracted Hawthorne. He was looking for weird stories to write, and he came to the Notch to meet the owner of the inn located at the Notch entrance, Ethan Allen Crawford.

Ethan was a giant of a man, a trail-blazing pioneer of the mountains. With his father Abel, he had built a small hotel to accommodate travelers who dared venture through the Notch. It was Ethan who also owned another little house in the middle of the Notch, which he had rented out to Sam Willey Jr. and his family some seven years earlier, setting the stage for the most brutal and unusual tragedy any White Mountains folks have ever experienced.

Even though there were settlements along the New Hampshire seacoast prior to the Pilgrims landing at Plymouth, Crawford Notch wasn't discovered by white settlers until 1771. Hunter Tim Nash just happened to climb a tree at Cherry Mountain to get his bearings one day, and spied this deep valley cut into the mountains. Tim followed the Saco River into the Notch and explored it, then reported his find to Governor Wentworth at Portsmouth. This pathway through the mountains to the North had been known by the Indians, but for over 100 years it was kept secret by them from the White Men. The Canadian Indians often used the Notch for surprise raids of New England's seaside villages. Upon being freed, kidnap victims began reporting that Indian raiding parties after capturing them, escaped through the mountains using this hidden narrow path which led them North and eventually into Canada.

Famous Indian fighter, Major Robert Rogers, was sent to Canada with 200 of his Rangers in 1759 to attack the Indian village of Saint Frances de Sales, just southwest of Quebec, and rescue many white New England captives. The Rangers attacked and massacred hundreds of Indians, burning their village. They also plundered the Catholic church at Saint Frances, carrying off silver plates, golden candlesticks, and a ten-pound silver image of the Virgin Mary. Retreating back to New England, the Rangers were pursued for twenty days by angry Indians. Rogers thought the men would make better time if they split into small groups and attempted to make their way through the mountains as best they could. The major and some of his men, after many days, made the fort at Charlestown, New Hampshire. But most of the other Rangers were tracked down, slaughtered and scalped by the Indians. A supposedly friendly Indian runner misled nine of the exhausted and starving Rangers, who carried the silver image into a secret dark passageway through the mountains. Today we know it as Crawford Notch. After poisoning one of them with a snake's fang, the Indian left the others, lost in a maze of mountains. Only one Ranger made it back to civilization. *"This ragged and forlorn looking mortal,"* Ethan Allen Crawford tells us, *"had with him six knives, and in his bloody knapsack was a piece of human flesh, which for the last eight days he declared he had eaten to support the flickering spark of life that now but faintly burned within him."* As to the plundered holy treasures, the golden candlesticks were found on the banks of Lake Memphremagog in 1816, but the ten-pound solid silver image of Mary has never been found.

When Tim Nash announced his discovery of the Notch in Portsmouth in 1771, the merchants were especially pleased, for now the mountains would not hinder trade with Northern and Western settlements. Nash and his fellow explorer, Ben Sawyer, were granted land in and around the Notch, if they could first prove that the Notch was passable for horses. This would establish a road from Portsmouth to the uplands of what the Indians called *"Cooes Country,"* along the Connecticut River. Nash and Sawyer transported a barrel of tobacco from Lancaster to the sea, and then a barrel of whiskey from Portsmouth to Lancaster. But Nash, Sawyer, and three other pioneers, who were to settle at the Notch, drank all the whiskey before it reached Lancaster. In fact, because of strong drink and poor judgements, Sawyer and Nash soon lost their claim to the land of the Notch. The Indians of the area also seemed to have *"great drunks,"* as Ethan Crawford called them. They carried their *"uncuppy"* whiskey with them at all times in moose bladders attached to their waist belts.

Ethan's grandparents, the Rosebrooks from Vermont, were the first to settle in the Notch area, and Hannah Rosebrook, Ethan's grandmother, was once attacked by a drunken Indian in her home. He aimed a tomahawk at her, and threatened to kill her *"but she gave him the evil eye"* says Ethan, and the Indian retreated. Ethan's father, Abel Crawford, to escape the wrath of his father-in-law, Elazar Rosebrook, traveled some 13 miles through the Notch to the other end and built his house, the Crawford House, as an inn for travelers. The first house in the Notch, was built in 1793, by a Nat Davis, Abel's son-in-law. Nat found the area too gloomy, being under the dark shadows of the mountains, so he left. The second house, later to be known as the *"Willey House,"* was built in the Notch by Henry Hill, an innkeeper, who hoped to attract visitors and merchants traveling between the Crawford House and the Rosebrooks, equally six miles away at either end of the Notch. Henry had few guests in the summer, and none in the winter, so the house was abandoned. In 1824, Ethan Crawford had plans to reopen the *"Notch House"*, as he called it, as a hostelry. He even hauled some hay down from Jefferson to the Notch House barn. But the snow piled deep in the Notch, and the winters seemed much colder and to last much longer than they did where he lived only six miles away, so he too gave up the idea.

In the autumn of 1825, Samuel Willey Jr., with his wife Polly Lovejoy Willey and their five children, moved into the old house in the Notch. Sam Willey was determined to make the Notch guesthouse work successfully. There was much repair work to be accomplished to the house, barn and outhouses before Sam Willey could open up his home as an inn for guests traveling through the Notch. He hired two live-in farmhands from North Conway to help him, Dave Nickerson and Dave Allen. The two Daves found the autumn scenery in the Notch as breathtaking as in their own village of Conway, but evening came too early each day. The steep purple peaks of the three surrounding mountains, Webster, Willard, and the third, soon to be named Willey, blocked out the sun in late afternoon. When the sun disappeared from the narrow valley, there was an unearthly silence in the air, even the birds ceased to chirp. Only the rush of the Saco River cut through the Notch, fifty yards away in a deep gulley, twenty feet below the house and barn. Towering 1,000 to 2,000 feet above and behind the house and barn were overhanging steep cliffs that became thick sheets of ice displaying giant blue dagger-like icicles during the winter months. The snows were deep, and the bone-chilling wind extremely brutal that first winter in the Notch. But the nine inhabitants of the Willey House suffered through until Spring. They had only a few adventurous overnight visitors, mostly businessmen who

Sam Willey surmised might have perished in snowstorms had not he and his family been there to feed, bed and board them.

When the weather cleared in May, more visitors passing through the Notch became overnight guests at the Willey House, and Sam predicted that his first year in the Notch would be financially successful. Polly, however, had a feeling of foreboding. The perpendicular wall of granite, dirt and pines that towered behind the house, frightened her. When the ice sheets melted, the crackling sounds unnerved her and the children, and occasionally a large boulder or a giant dripping icicle would bounce or shatter into their back yard.

It seemed to the Willeys that there was no Spring in the Notch. Winter melted quickly into Summer, with hot sultry days and little rain. One day in late June, 1826, while Abel Crawford and some other men were making repairs on the road near the Willey House, a sudden torrent of rain forced them to duck into the house. Welcomed by Sam and Polly, just inside, they all heard a tremendous roar outside from somewhere above their heads. *"We saw on the west side of the road, a small movement of rocks and earth, coming down the hill,"* reported Abel Crawford, *"and it took all before it. We saw likewise, whole trees coming down the hill standing upright, for ten rods together, before they would tip over—the whole still moving slowly on, making its way until it had crossed the road, and then on a level surface some distance before it stopped. This grand and awful sight frightened the family very much."*

Although this landslide did not come near the house, Polley Willey and her offspring wanted to leave immediately, but Sam persuaded her and the children to stay. He promised to keep a wagon with a team of horses at the ready at all times, if they but heard a slight rumble from the mountains. He also built a sturdy shelter near the river in case they would ever have to abandon the house for fear of an avalanche. Polly reluctantly remained in the house, but her younger children with the family dog, shivered and cried for hours after they witnessed their first landslide and heard it echo terribly throughout the valley on that hot and rainy June afternoon. The next few weeks were uneventful but for the intense heat and the lack of rain. The Willey family forgot their fears of the mountains falling on them, although occasionally stones bounced off their roof.

Monday, August 28th, the day dawned hot and dry, like the many days before, but by late morning, an ominous mist covered the mountain peaks. By noon, dark clouds loomed above, lightening flashed and thunder roared. The two Daves locked the oxen, horses and sheep into the barn, and as sheets of rain poured into the Notch, they made their way to the house to sit out the storm with the Willey family. It was a wild storm that raged all day and well into the night. The river rose over the road and started making its way up to the house. Rocks began falling around the house from the high cliffs above, a few hitting the roof. The mountains began to shake. Sam Willey had everyone gather their chairs around the hearth, where a blazing fire not only kept out the dampness, but added a touch of coziness to the nightmare that surrounded them. Water reached the front door and started seeping into the house. More rocks and earth fell with a rumble and roar from 1,000 feet above their heads. The dog whimpered and howled; the children cried and screamed. Polly wept and the farmhands trembled. Sam opened the Bible to the Eighteenth Psalm: *"The Lord also thundered,"* he read aloud, *"in the heavens.... Hailstones and coals of fire, He sent from above.... He took me, He drew me out of many waters...."* Sam was shouting, but Polly and the children and the two Daves couldn't hear him. It sounded like the whole mountain was coming down on them.

Meanwhile, six miles away at the Crawford House, the river rose high enough to drown 24 of Ethan Crawford's sheep and to destroy Abel's saw-mill. At daylight, Ethan's little boy Harvey cried *"the earth is covered with water and the hogs are swimmin for their lives."* All of the Crawfords' farm crops were ruined by the rising river and torrential rains. When the sky cleared, the Crawfords were so busy with their own tragedy that they had no time to think of the Willeys in the Notch. But an overnight guest, John Barker, traveling from Whitefield to Bridgeton, Maine, borrowed Ethan Crawford's horse and plodded through rubble and flooded road hoping to spend the night after the storm at the Willey House. Barker made it to the house hungry and exhausted, just as darkness was setting in. Welcoming smoke was curling out of the Willey House chimney into the cool damp air. But when Barker entered the house, there was not a soul to greet him, not even the friendly Willey dog. Embers smoldered in the fireplace and nine empty chairs circled the hearth. Money and papers were spread out on the bar, and the Bible was opened to the Eighteenth Psalm. Barker concluded that the Willeys and their farmhands were either out inspecting the damage from the storm, or frightened by the high waters, they fled to relatives, possibly to Sam Willey's father's home in Bartlett. John Barker grabbed a quick snack from the kitchen, layed down on the living room couch and fell asleep.

He was awakened in the middle of the night by a painful moaning sound coming from just outside the house. It was not a human voice, but a gutteral, inhuman groan that persisted through the night, frightening Barker so that he couldn't sleep yet didn't dare move from the couch. At dawn he garnered enough courage to investigate. The moaning was coming from the barn which had collapsed during the storm. Caught under a roof-beam was an old ox with a broken horn. Barker managed to free the wounded animal.

It wandered off through the rubble in a daze, still moaning. In the daylight Barker noticed that rocks, mud, and splintered trees stacked some twenty feet high surrounded the house. They had crushed all the surrounding sheds and outbuildings. There had been a devastating landslide from the mountainside behind the house. The avalanche had apparently split into two sections as it rushed down the steep cliffs, separated by a large overhanging boulder directly behind the house. Oozing debris, rocks and rubble to either side and far beyond the house, it not so much as splintered a shingle or shattered a window in the house.

Barker thought it strange that the house was abandoned, but still believed the occupants had escaped to another inn in the mountains, or to a relative's house. He left the Willey House and traveled on down the Notch, where he observed the Saco River had risen some twenty feet in certain sections. But as he inquired of others along the road, no one had seen any members of the Willey family. Barker decided to travel to Bartlett to Sam Willey's father's house, to see if the family might have gone there. Sam Willey, Sr., hadn't seen or heard from any of them. The seven Willeys and the two farmhands had disappeared, but the family dog had been seen. Miles away from the Willey House, it came howling and whining to the Lovejoys' house, the home of Polly Willey's mother and father. Mrs. Lovejoy reported the dog arrived there on Tuesday, the day after the storm, *"but when I approached it, it would cower away, but it returned later, howling at the top of its lungs. It tried to make people understand what had taken place,"* said Mrs. Lovejoy, *"but not succeeding, it left. The dog was afterwards seen frequently on the road between the Notch house and our home, sometimes heading north, and sometimes south, running almost at top speed, as though bent on some important errand, but it soon disappeared from this region and has never been seen since."*

Ben Willey, Sam's brother, organized a search party. With the help of the Crawfords, they began clearing away the debris from around the Willey House on Wednesday, two days after the storm. The mangled body of Polly Willey was found, clutching her crushed child, only a few feet from the front door of the house under a large boulder that took seven men to move. Next day Dave Allen's body was found near the house, also under a large boulder that had tumbled 1,000 feet down the mountainside. Sam Willey Jr.'s twisted body was found by the river two days later. And Sally Willey, five years old, the youngest of the Willey children was fished out of the Saco River that following Sunday. Farmhand Dave Nickerson's body was discovered near the house under 20 feet of rubble a few days later. Three of the Willey children, two boys and a girl, were never found. Even today, one wonders if they perished under the crushing earth and rocks of the avalanche. Or like the family dog, did they escape to wander the mountain wilderness in panic and shock?

With the house unscathed by the avalanche and untouched by the flood—although there was some evidence that the flooding river had entered the first floor of the house—why did all nine of the occupants leave to meet the devastation of both the avalanche and the flood outside the house? The only answer is that fear overwhelmed them. A blinding thunder and lightning storm; a rising river at their doorstep; and an avalanche of rocks, earth and splintered pines roaring down from above. Their little world was literally crashing in on them from all sides, and they fled in panic. Had they remained with their Bible by the hearth, they would have lived. As Nat Hawthorne explained it in his fictionalized *"Twice Told Tales,"* they *"quitted their security and fled right into the pathway of destruction."*

The Willey House was abandoned for eighteen years after this terrible tragedy, yet *"the romantic pass of the Notch,"* as Hawthorne called it, became more popular than ever, *"as a great artery, through which the life-blood of internal commerce continuously throbbed between Maine on one side, and the Green Mountains and the shores of St. Lawrence on the other."* But when passing the old Willey House, travelers would bow their heads and sometimes add a boulder or two to a pyramid-like monument by the road near the house, under which, it was said, Polly Willey and two of her children were buried in a makeshift grave.

In 1844, the house was repaired and reopened as a hotel. Nat Hawthorne was on his way to spend the night there in May of 1864, with his old college chum and former President of the United States, Franklin Pierce. They only made it as far as the Pemigewasset House in Plymouth, New Hampshire. There, Nat Hawthorne died in his sleep. The old Willey House mysteriously burned to the ground in 1898.

The Willey House in Crawford Notch, New Hampshire, prior to 1826.

III
Those Frigid Vermonters

Vermont is a beautiful state, possibly the prettiest of America's fifty, but few people live there, and one must wonder why it does not entice more residents. The answer is the cold. The majestic Green Mountains and lush green valleys of Vermont, are grey or snow covered for much of the year, and with the chilling winds that sweep down from Canada, the temperature often drops to well below zero. They've had more than one winter where the temperature dropped to thirty-five degrees below zero and remained there for almost two weeks. Over a foot of snow fell in Vermont in June of 1816, and Lake Champlain was frozen for many weeks during that summer. One, therefore, has only to imagine what it would be like to endure an average long winter in Vermont.

New Englanders have been noted throughout history for having cold dispositions, not open and friendly like Southerners or Californians. This image of frigidity seems to have lessened of late, but Vermonters hold tightly to tradition. Even one of their two contributions to the Presidency of these United States, Calvin Coolidge, was described by the *New York Times* as *"cold as an iceberg."* The *Times* also displayed a headline during Coolidge's reign, which read: *"PRESIDENT NEARLY LAUGHS."* A friend of the droopy-mouthed President said *"he was weaned on a pickle, and is from Vermont, where everything is cold."* During his presidency there was even a story circulating in Washington D.C., that the Coolidge family derived its surname from the macabre practice of placing the family elders into cold-storage during the winter months in Vermont, to save on food expenses. They then were thawed from their long sleep in the Spring, *"so's they could help with the planting."*

Although we accept the fact that some animals hibernate during the winter months, the fact that Vermonters, especially the unproductive elderly, were induced into hibernation in Vermont, was a shock to this nation, when it was revealed in the *"Montpelier Argus & Patriot,"* in December of 1887. The man who uncovered this sinister secret, used only his initials, "A.M.," and obviously opted to remain anonymous because of the horror it evoked:

"I am an old man," he began his story, *"and have seen some strange sights in the course of a roving life in foreign lands, as well as in this country, but none so strange as one found recorded in an old diary, kept by my Uncle William, that came into my possession a few years ago, at his decease."* The diary read as follows: *"January 7—I went on the mountain today and witnessed what to me was a horrible sight. It seems that the dwellers there,*

who are unable either from age or other reasons to contribute to the support of their families, are disposed of in the winter months in a manner that will shock the one who reads this diary, unless the person lives in that vicinity....

"Six persons, four men and two women, the man a cripple about thirty years old, the other five past the age of usefulness, lay on the earthly floor of the cabin, drugged into insensibility, while members of the family were gathered about them in apparent indifference. In a short time, the unconscious bodies were inspected by several people who announced they were ready. They were then stripped of all their clothing except for a single garment. The bodies were carried outside and laid on logs, exposed to the bitter cold mountain air, the operation having been delayed several days for suitable weather....

"Soon the noses, ears and fingers began to turn white, then the limbs and faces assumed a tallowy look. I could stand the cold no longer and went inside, where I found the friends in cheerful conversation. In about an hour I went out and looked at the bodies. They were fast freezing. I went back inside....I could not shut out the sight of their freezing bodies outside....

"January 8—Day came at length and did not dissipate the terror that filled me. The frozen bodies became visibly white on the snow that lay in huge drifts about them. The women gathered about the fire and soon commenced preparing breakfast. The men awoke, and conversation again commencing, affairs assumed a more cheerful aspect. After breakfast the men lighted their pipes and some of them took a yoke of oxen and went off toward the forest, while others proceeded to nail together boards making a box about ten-feet long and half as high and wide. When this was completed they placed about two feet of straw in the bottom. Then they laid three frozen bodies on the straw. Then the faces and upper part of the bodies were covered with a cloth and straw. Boards were then firmly nailed on top to protect the bodies from being injured by carniverous animals that made their home on these mountains. By this time the men who went off with the ox-team returned with a huge load of spruce and hemlock boughs which they unloaded at the foot of a steep ledge, came to the house and loaded the box containing the bodies on the sled and drew it to the foot of the ledge near the load of boughs. These were soon piled on and around the box and it was left to be covered with snow which I was told would lay in drifts twenty feet deep over this rude tomb.

'We shall want our men to plant our corn next Spring,' said a youngish-looking woman, the wife of one of the frozen men, 'If you want to see them resuscitated you come back here about the tenth of next May.'

"May 10—I arrived here, twenty miles outside Montpelier, at 10 A.M. after riding about four hours over muddy, unsettled roads. The weather here is warm and pleasant, most of the snow is gone except here and there. There are drifts in the fence corners and hollows, but nature is not yet dressed in green. I found the same parties here I left last January, ready to disinter the bodies of their friends. I had no expectations of finding any life there, but a feeling that I could not resist, impelled me to come and see.

"We repaired at once to the well remembered spot at the ledge. The snow had melted from the top of the brush, but still lay deep around the bottom of the pile. The men commenced work at once, some shoveling, and others tearing away the brush. Soon the box was visible. The cover was taken off, the layers of straw removed and the bodies, frozen and apparently lifeless, lifted out and laid on the snow. Large troughs made out of hemlock logs were placed nearby filled with tepid water, into which the bodies were placed separately with the head slightly raised. Boiling water was then poured into the troughs from kettles hung on poles nearby, until the water was as hot as I could hold my hand in. Hemlock boughs had been put in the boiling water in such quantity that they had given the water the color of wine.

"After lying in the bath about an hour, color began to return to the bodies, when all hands began rubbing and chafing them. This continued about an hour, when a slight twitching of the muscles of the face and limbs, followed by audible gasps, showed that life was not quenched and that vitality was returning. Spirits were then given in small quantities and allowed to trickle down their throats. Soon they could swallow and more was given them. Then their eyes opened and they began to talk. They finally sat up in their bathtubs. They were taken out and assisted to the house, where after a hearty meal they seemed as well as ever and in no wise injured, but rather refreshed by their long sleep of four months. Truly, truth is stranger than fiction."

Most Vermonters, of course, deny that the above story is true. But I have visited Vermont in early Spring and have found that many old-timers there had not yet completely thawed out. If you stop one of them on the road to ask for information or directions, they will often stare into space or look dumbfounded, and any other statement will be answered with only one word, either a "EEY-UP" or a "AH-NOPE". I suggest you don't visit Vermont until June or July when the inhabitants are fully recovered from the previous winter. I further advise that you don't enter Vermont after mid-October—the foliage season is usually over then—for this is when they begin to contemplate hibernation. Obviously, if you are over 65 years of age, it would be best to avoid Vermont altogether, especially when it is cold and snowy, which could be at any time throughout the year.

IV
Gold In Them Thar Hills

Gold mines, silver mines, and diamond mines in the New England mountains, their locations supposedly kept secret by the Indians, were the reason why fortune hunters, often disguised as explorers, fishermen and trappers, come to the New World from Europe. At the first English settlement in Maine in 1607, Pilgrim Thomas Hanham reported to London, *"some oare was found in this country that did prove to be silver."* Sir Ferinando Gorges, sponsor of many expeditions to New England, including the plantation settlement at Plymouth, interviewed and badgered many captured Indians, offering them freedom if they would tell him where their gold mines were located. One clever Indian chief who was captured at Cape Cod and shipped to England, told Sir Gorges that he would show the White Men the gold mine, if he was allowed to return to his people.

"Hidden Gold," said Chief Epanow, *"is North of my island of Chapwick,"* which is known today as Martha's Vineyard. Under the protective custody of English Captain Holson and his crew, Epanow, *"with every precaution taken to prevent his escape,"* was brought back to Cape Cod. Twenty canoes filled with armed Indians met Holson's ship as it approached the island, and *"Epanow, knocking away two guards, leaped overboard and swam to a canoe, as the savages showered us with arrows."* For many years thereafter, Chief Epanow and his tribe revenged his capture by attacking white settlers and explorers who ventured too close to Martha's Vineyard, and Sir Gorges never did find out where the Indian gold mine was hidden. Historians today believe that Epanow only used the gold mine story to get passage back to New England. Yet, rumor persisted throughout the 1600's and 1700's that the Indians worked a secret gold mine somewhere in the mountains.

It wasn't until the early 1800's that gold was discovered in New England, in the Swift River, at what is now, Byron, Maine, near Old Blue Mountain and Tumbledown Mountain, bordering New Hampshire. Today, tourists and locals alike still successfully pan for gold in Maine's Swift River. Also, small quantities of gold nuggets have been found near the Maine state line in New Hampshire's Pemigewasset River. Gold was discovered at Lisbon, New Hampshire at Sugar Hill in 1864, and a mine was opened, producing almost $100,000 in gold bars. But more than that was spent in manpower and equipment to get it out. Ten years later, gold was found at Dublin, New Hampshire on Monadnock Mountain, and a mine was opened there, but the gold vein diminished and the mine was closed soon after the initial discovery.

Returning home from the California goldrush of 1849, some Vermont miners started chipping away at the Green Mountains, especially around Plymouth and Bridgewater, which, to the prospectors, resembled the fruitful California gold hills. There were no great strikes, but gold was found and mines were opened up. Some continue to dig sucessfully for gold and pan the streams in the Green Mountains today. There was also a goldrush that petered out in the late 1800's in the Berkshire Mountains of Western Massachusetts. And a quantity of gold was found, but not enough to whet the appetites of those who wanted to *"strike it rich."* The greatest treasure found in the Berkshires, at a coldwater spring near Adams, Massachusetts, was a large, very valuable diamond. That was in 1825, and to my knowledge, not one other natural diamond has been found anywhere in New England before or since.

Silver, and not gold or diamonds, has caused the greatest controversy and treasure lure in New England, especially in Vermont. Yet experts say, *"there is no silver in Vermont!"* The most successful silver mine opened in 1881 at Mount Hayes near Gorham, New Hampshire. Many silver veins were discovered there and great quantities of ore were removed and sold. The price of silver, though, didn't justify the cost of operation, and the Mascot Mine of Mount Hayes was closed in the early 1900s.

Brandon is about 23 miles from Bristol, Vermont, and Pittsford is some 11 miles from Brandon. It is then 20 miles on Route 7 from Pittsford to Wallingford, Vermont, and another 25 or more miles southeast from Wallingford to Chester. Yet all these towns lay claim to Vermont's famous *"Lost Spanish Silver Mine."* The unfound hoard of silver, hidden in the mountains by Spaniards, is part of the folklore in each of the aforementioned towns, although the stories differ, depending on which town or village you're in, and who's telling the story. I am a great believer in the saying, *"where there is smoke there is fire,"* and *"where there is a folktale, there is some hidden truth that sparked the tale."* I will summarize each town's tale, and save what I think may be the true story until last.

At Chester, Vermont, they will tell you that an old man on horseback came out of the mountains one day in the autumn of the year 1800. His saddlebags were bulging with silver bars. Speaking with a Spanish acent, he told some villagers he had taken the bars from a silvermine *"in the white rocks, two miles East of North Wallingford Center."*

At Wallingford and at Brandon too, you'll hear the same story. But it happened in the late 1700's, and the Spaniard was not on horseback, and he had no silver with him. He came into town from his hidden silver mine, after being attacked by Indians. In Brandon, the story deviates a bit. *Their* Spaniard is not a minor, but a counterfeiter, and two of his thieving partners were killed by the Indians. In Pittsford, a man named DeGrau, who had been digging for silver alone in the mountains, wandered into a country store, stating that he had found a vast quantity of silver, had melted it into crude bars or ingots, and then buried it, fearing the Indians would get it. He left for Spain to get needed funds to start up a silver mining company, but died there. The location of his hidden silver is unknown to this day.

I like the Bristol story best. It was written up in the *Bristol Herald* by Franklin Harvey in 1889:

Just after the Revolutionary War, three Spaniards who were experts at mining precious metals in Central America, came exploring South Mountain and found rich veins of silver. They left the site for almost a year, and returned with the necessary equipment, two women, and a little boy. The boy's name was Philip DeGrau. Digging into the white cliffs, they uncovered so much silver that they smelted it into silver bars and stacked the bars in a nearby cave.

"We were constantly pestered by wild animals, especially wolves," Philip DeGrau later reported, *"and local Indians snooped about to see what we were doing."* One of the two women died of a sickness that autumn and the men weighted her body down with stones and dropped her into a nearby pond, so the wolves wouldn't dig up her body. When the snow started to fall, the miners decided to leave and return the following Spring. They had mined so much silver that they couldn't carry it out, so they placed their tools in the nearby cave with the silver bars, rocked in the cave entrance, plastered it with mud and moss to hide the location from the Indians, and returned to Spain. *"They vowed to each other that none of them would return to the site without the others,"* but as Philip DeGrau later reported, *"one miner died in Spain that Winter, another refused to return, and the third miner couldn't afford the passage back to America."*

The little boy, Philip DeGrau, returned some 18 years later in the year 1800, and attempted to find the hidden cave at South Mountain. The town of Bristol was called by the Indian name Pocook then, and there were only a few homesteads. DeGrau remembered that there was a pond about 100 yards west of the silver mine, and a river ran about a mile and a half away from the cave with the hidden silver bars and tools. Still, after months of searching, he couldn't find it again. He remained in the mountains searching for almost a year, coming into Bristol to buy food supplies. He finally gave up. During his last night in town, he told the store proprietor about cutting alders for the miners when he was a boy, to produce the charcoal for smelting, and that the alders grew only near the river. The proprietor knew this was true. *"Maybe I've been searching in the wrong spot,"* were

Philip DeGrau's final words at Bristol, *"but I think not."* The proprietor thought he might return the following Spring. He didn't.

Hundreds, from that day to this, have searched Bristol Cliffs, South Mountain, Bloodroot Mountain and Whiterocks Mountain for the Spanish silver mine and the cave of silver bars. They remain unfound. Miners have dug shafts over the years, honeycombing the cliffs with holes and yawing caves, to the extent that a part of South Mount is called *"Hell's Half Acre,"* because of all the holes. A commercial venture in 1840 was started by a group of Canadians. After their efforts failed, they departed the area leaving more deep scars in the mountain. Some of these man-made shafts plunge over 100 feet into the rock, making it a dangerous place to visit. Early in this century a boy fell into one of the cave-like holes and wasn't found for two weeks. His body was discovered after his loyal dog was found dead at the entrance of the shaft. Today that shaft is called, *"The Ghost Shaft of South Mountain."* Possibly the boy was looking for the lost silver mine when he fell in. Nobody knows.

On cold wintry nights, residents of Bristol often hear the howling of a dog from way up on the mountain side, coming, they believe, from the Ghost Shaft where the boy's body was found. I don't know if the story of the lost Spanish silver mine is true or not, but it certainly gives Vermonters something to ponder and talk about during those notoriously long cold winters.

Many mountainmen of today carry metal-detectors instead of weapons, as they search for lost silver mines. Here, Allan Janard of New Durham, New Hampshire hunts for the Lost Spanish Silver Mine at Bristol, Vermont.

V
The Snow Ghost Of Conway

It was Bill Ryan, owner of a ski-cabin in North Conway, New Hampshire, who initiated my investigation into the story of a ghost that rides the mountain ranges on a snowmobile up in that neck of the woods. *"Few have actually seen the ghost rider,"* Bill informed me, *"but on a blustery, snowy night, when no sane person would stir from hearth and home,"* said Bill, *"the whine of a snowmobile can be heard in the distance, and a faint glow can be seen in the mountains, traveling at great speed across the steep ridges. It's an eerie sight, and the echoing, haunting sound, can send a chill down your spine."*

Bill, who was once the Mayor of Haverhill, Massachusetts, likes to joke a lot, so I thought his snowmobiling ghost of the Conways, was just another of his tall tales. That is, until I met famous movie producer and writer Victor Pisano of Martha's Vineyard. Pisano grew up in Connecticut, and we met in Salem while working on his television mini-series, *"Three Sovereigns For Sarah."* One afternoon, while sitting around the movie-tent between takes, we got onto the subject of ghosts, and I mentioned that Bill Ryan had seen a ghost on a snowmobile from his cabin window on a stormy night in North Conway. Vic Pisano said he knew the story behind the snowmobile ghost and that it was true. Not only was the ghost seen in Conway but in the Berkshire Mountains as well. *"The story begins, strangely enough,"* said Vic, *"in my home town of Monroe, Connecticut, and concerns a large family named Pudeater. I, in fact, went to school with some of the Pudeater boys."* Victor then proceeded to tell me one of the most tragic and humorous ghost stories I have ever heard. So I pass it on to you unedited, just as he told it to me.

"Pa Pudeater died, and Ma Pudeater, a sprightly old gal with a constant twinkle in her eye, was matriarch of the family. Ma and Pa Pudeater had six burly sons, and they all lived on scattered farms around Monroe. Their yards were kind of like junkyards, with old discarded bathtubs, automobiles and other things strewn about. There were a lot of domestic farm animals around, too. Mostly cattle. Some with skins, some without. The Pudeaters, you see, kept the carcasses and skins of their slaughtered cattle in the old bathtubs! The six sons married, and they had children, so there was a large assortment of Pudeaters about. I was fourteen years old at the time, and very impressionable, and I thought it weird that some of the Pudeater boys had to be in bed by 6:30 p.m. There were so many of them that they had to eat and sleep in shifts. They were relatively poor, but an industrious lot, and besides cattle and junk, I believe they were in some sort

of oil distribution business.

"*I remember it was around December, 1959, that the boys were all excited because three of the Pudeater men and two of their sons decided to pool what little extra money they had to buy a new contraption called a snowmobile. This was a big decision for them, for snowmobiles were very expensive. But they purchased it and a flatbed trailer as well, to tow the snowmobile behind their pick-up truck. A friend of theirs owned an old cabin with an outhouse in Conway, New Hampshire, and three of Ma Pudeater's oldest sons, and two of her grandsons, decided to drive to Conway to try out the snowmobile. Ma was all excited about the snowmobile, but when the boys tried to have her drive it for a short spin in the yard, she got a little timid and said she was too old, but that she might give it a try once all the boys got used to it. It was then that the boys asked Ma if she wanted to drive up to Conway with them. She rarely left her home, and the boys felt that this would be a real treat for her. Even those Pudeaters who were to stay behind in Monroe, thought it would be a nice change for Ma—like a little vacation. She finally agreed. Her three oldest sons, two teenaged grandsons, and Ma, headed off in two pick-up trucks with the trailer carrying the snowmobile in tow behind one pick-up. It took them seven hours of driving before they arrived at the desolate cabin. It was late afternoon, but the boys were anxious to try out the snowmobile in a pasture they spotted coming in, some 15 miles from the cabin.*

'*You go ahead boys,' Ma said. 'I'll tidy up here and have supper ready for you in a few hours when you come back.' So, off they went, and truly enjoyed what was left of the afternoon, riding the snowmobile over hill and dale, two at a time, then returning back to the trucks so that two more Pudeater boys could roar off at great speed into the snow covered countryside. It started to snow quite heavily when the last two took their turn. And then the new snowmobile conked out when they were almost a half mile from the trucks. It was dark by the time they towed it back, and the snow was falling fast and piling up as they tried to repair the snowmobile and get it going again. When they decided to head back to the cabin, their trucks began slipping and sliding in the snow, and the trailer with the snowmobile on it just couldn't plow through the heavy accumulation. They were now in the middle of a blizzard and out in the middle of nowhere, without a house around. The Pudeater boys were survivalists, and even though they were snowed in, with temperatures dropping well below zero, they were confident in their own abilities to make do. Thirty inches of snow fell that night and throughout the following day. And the temperature dropped even lower. It was three days before the boys got out, one of them trudging through five miles of knee-deep snow to get help.*

"The two boys, during their ordeal said they were worried about Ma, all alone in the cabin, but Ma's three sons thought that she was resourceful enough to take care of herself. Besides, there was nothing they could do for her while they were stuck in the blizzard. When they made it back to the cabin and shouted for Ma before they forced open the front door, there was no response from inside. When they entered, a sad sight greeted them— there was poor old Ma, sitting in a rocking chair before the cold wood-burning stove. She was frozen solid, a shawl and blanket tucked tight about her scrawny body. She had apparently run out of firewood, and there was no food left in the cabin. Evidently, though, she died peacefully, for there was a little half-smile on her blue lips. The sons, especially her grandsons, went wild with anguish and grief. The oldest boy tried to move her to a bed, but rigormortis had set in and they couldn't pry her fingers from the arms of the rocking chair. When they were finally able to lift her out of the chair, she was in a permanent L position. They set her on the couch, and went to get the coroner. The appropriate papers were filed, but they didn't have the money to have a mortician ship her body back to Monroe. So, they decided to take her back with them in one of the trucks for an appropriate burial in Monroe.

"It was easy to fit Ma into the pick-up in her sitting position, but none of them wanted to take the long ride back to Connecticut with Ma sitting beside them. So it was decided to sit her on the snowmobile and strap her in. 'She finally got her ride on that snowmobile,' one of the teenagers wept, which set them all to bawling again. They threw a tarp over Ma and the snow- mobile, tied that down to the trailer, and began their long sad trek back home.

"They rode along through New Hampshire and Massachusetts, none of the boys talking much, although the youngest shouted aloud once, 'We killed Ma'! And the other grandson moaned about what the rest of the fam- ily would feel and think once they arrived home. At "Bernie's Place," a log- cabin eatery in the Berkshires, just outside Pittsfield, the boys pulled off the road to hit the men's-room, grab a bite to eat, and have a couple of beers. Inside Bernie's, country music was playing, and that started tears and moans all over again, for it was Ma's favorite music. They sat, drank, ate, argued, drank some more, and cried when a sad song played on the jukebox. It was almost two hours before they left Bernie's, ready for the last lap of their journey home. They climbed into their pick-up trucks, and then realized that something was missing.

"The trailer was gone! Someone in a vehicle must have unhitched the trailer from their pick-up and drove off with it in tow and the snowmobile with Ma still sitting on it! The boys went berserk. Four of them raced around the Berkshires in their pick-ups searching for the thief, without success. The two oldest sons went to the police, but the police couldn't find the stolen trailer and snowmobile with Ma sitting on it either. After two days of searching and severe mental anquish, the Pudeater boys returned to Monroe and told the rest of the family the story. The trailer, snowmobile, and Ma, were never found. Imagine the shock of the thief or thieves after removing the canvas, coming face-to-face with Ma's frozen half-smile! This," Vic Pisano swears, "is a true story."

After hearing this story from Vic, I passed it on to Bill Ryan. As he sits by his cabin window facing the snowy mountains at North Conway, Bill hears that faraway whine of a snowmobile and he sees the eerie glow on the snowcrested rocky ridges. But, Bill now knows that the ghost-rider plowing through the snow is old Ma Pudeater, a smile creasing her cracked lips, her white straggly hair blowing in the wind, as she enjoys her first and last ride on that eternal snowmobile in the sky.

The haunted Hoosac Tunnel that cuts under the Mohawk Trail.

VI
The Haunted Hoosac Tunnel

I was driving through the mountains of Western Massachusetts, one of the most breathtaking drives in New England, especially in the autumn at peak foliage time. Although I must admit that I am partial to the Maine seacoast in all seasons, in the autumn, however, this old Mohawk Indian trail is the most spectacular, multi-colored sight in the world. Here, Massachusetts, New York and Vermont meet, dipping from the Hoosac Mountains, to the Connecticut and Deerfield Valleys. A thick fog covered the mountain this day, and not wanting to manuever the hair-pin turns in the fog, I pulled off the road at the Eastern Summit Giftshop. Entering the shop, a cloud of white mist followed at my heels. I commented to the man at the gift-counter that the cloud looked like a ghost following me.

"No ghosts around here," he said, *"too high up for them."*

I introduced myself to Joe Devanney, owner of the shop. I told him that I couldn't believe such a desolate, deep forested place didn't have ghosts. A damp, misty day like this along the seacoast was ideal weather for brooding specters. Joe Devanney insisted that there were no ghosts in the mountains, *"but directly below us,"* he informed me, pointing down through the floorboards of the shop, *"at the base of the mountain, some say that the Hoosac Tunnel is haunted."*

I had heard of the Hoosac Tunnel, but didn't know much about it. From my prior research of Indians, I did know that *"Hoosac"* was an Indian name, meaning *"people of the long house,"* and that it was a name other Indian tribes gave to the Iroquois nation, of which the Mohawks were part. The tunnel, I had been told, was a railroad tunnel that ran for five miles directly through the mountains from one valley to another.

"It took over one-thousand men some twenty-five years of digging and blasting to complete the tunnel," said Joe. *"Some of the young vigorous workers who started the project back in 1851, were worn and grey-haired when the tunnel was completed in 1876, and about two-hundred of them lost their lives in the tunnel."*

"So, it's these dead workers that haunt the tunnel?"

"I don't know," Joe said, *"but some people say they can see a dull glow inside the tunnel, looking in from the entrance, and it's impossible to see all the way to the other end, so they concluded that it's a ghost living in there."* He smiled.

I told Joe that I'd like to visit the tunnel, and he directed me to *"take the next side road to the right off the Trail, just before you get to Whitcomb Summit Observation Tower, then bear right down an old dirt road and head straight down to the bottom of the mountain, then take a sharp left and you'll come to it."*

I thanked him, got back into my car and started out to find the entrance to the Hoosac Tunnel. When I turned off the Mohawk Trail at Whitcomb Summit and headed down, there was a hand-printed sign by the road that I couldn't read because of the dense fog. Hours later, when I returned to the summit and the sun had broken through the haze, I could read the sign: *"Road Washed Out—Do Not Enter."* Once on the dirt road, it was like a bumpy roller-coaster ride with such a spectacular view down the side of the mountain that it made me dizzy. Then I came to the spot where the road had been eaten away by a flooded stream, with a fall of some 2,000 feet of sheer rock cliffs if I didn't properly manuever the car around the washout. I had come this far to find the tunnel, so I wasn't about to turn around. Even to attempt turning around at this point seemed more dangerous to me than to squeeze by the gaping hole in the road. I made it, and kept heading down, my foot pumping the break, not daring to take my eyes off the narrow, winding road to look at the scenery—I hadn't seen a house, another vehicle, or another human being on the way down.

When I got to flat land, there was a sign pointing in the *"sharp left"* direction, that Joe Devanney had told me to go. The sign read: *"Bear Swamp,"* and that didn't sound too appealing to me. The little road seemed to lead into swampland, but after my hair-raising descent from the mountaintop, I wasn't about to turn back. The sun was peeking through the clouds as I drove on, and I noticed that railroad tracks ran parrallel to the road. I saw a little patch of cleared out weeds off to the side of the road, and some large rock structure near the tracks beyond. Joe had said that I would have to walk the tracks for about fifty yards to come to the tunnel entrance, so I pulled off the road, and with camera in hand, started walking down the weed covered tracks. Looming up before me, with ragged cliffs, mica slates, and pine trees climbing straight up the sides, for thousands of feet, was the fort-like entrance to the Hoosac Tunnel. It was an imposing, eerie portal, with a 24-foot oval of darkness into which the rusty tracks ran. Five miles away, through this dank and gloomy looking tunnel, was the Hoosic River, which led on to Albany and Troy, New York.

As I walked towards the tunnel, I began feeling jittery, as if everything was closing in, around and above me. There was a faint light inside the tunnel—a dull, quivering green glow. My first thought was that a train was coming at me through the tunnel, yet the light didn't seem to be coming closer. Maybe it's a signal light located a few hundred feet inside the tunnel, I thought. But if trains didn't run constantly in or out, why would there be a light inside? I had an urge to walk the tracks toward the light, but I thought better of it. I backed off a bit to take a photo, but then I saw and heard something rustling in the brush beside the tracks about fifty feet ahead. An animal, I thought. Maybe one of those bears from Bear Swamp. I looked around, just in case I was right, but there was no place for me to run. Then I saw that the thing in the bushes was wearing something red—a red jacket. A man with a camera emerged. Strange, I thought, that at the same time as I, someone else had the same idea to photograph the entrance to the Hoosac Tunnel out here in the wilderness. *"Guess our minds are running on the same track today,"* I shouted over to him. He waved and walked over. His name was Felten, and the coincidence of our meeting in such a desolate place was further intensified when he told me he was *"a member of the Boston & Maine Historical Society, headquartered at Howard Station, Littleton, Massachusetts."*

"You're just the man I need to answer my many questions about this tunnel," I said. *"First I want to know what that green glow is inside the tunnel?"* I pointed into the darkness, and Mister Felten stared. He saw it too. *"Might be a signal indicator,"* he said, squinting into the tunnel at the prick of light, *"but I don't think it is."*

"Is it a ghost then?" He gave me a strange look, as if I might be demented. I laughed. *"I hear the tunnel is haunted,"* I said.

"I've heard that too," he replied, *"but I don't think that's a ghost."*

"Probably not," I agreed, *"but I'd really like to know why people think the tunnel is haunted."*

"There is one ghost story that Carl Byron, the head of our society, tells about the tunnel," said Mr. Felten, as he stared quizzically at the green light, and he proceeded to tell the story.

"From the day the tunnel was completed, a man was hired as a track-walker," said Felton, *"who each day walked the tunnel from one end to the other and back, removing rocks that fell on the tracks, or chasing out wild animals such as deer that often wandered into the tunnel. The track-walkers, working in shifts, were Italian immigrants, as were most of the men who dug the tunnel,"* said Felton. *"There was a train accident about half-way into the tunnel only a few years after it opened. Two freight-trains collided. It was after this accident that the Italian track-walkers started seeing ghosts as they made their rounds."*

Track-walker Antonio Alberti came screaming out of the East-portal one day. Trembling, he climbed to the control-tower, where Amos Writter operated the board. Antonio, in broken English, explained to Amos that he had not seen just one ghost in the tunnel, but three. At first they were just *"white flashes"* dancing in and out of his lantern light, but then he saw one of their *"ugly faces"* and heard its sinister laugh. Amos, a conservative old Yankee, decided to see for himself. He headed into the tunnel with a smoke-lantern, with Alberti close at his heels. About two miles in, both men started seeing the white flashes, just beyond the glow of their lanterns. Amos stopped in his tracks and swung the lantern back and forth. Solid white forms appeared, darting nimbly from one side of the tracks to the other. Antonio was right, but Amos controlled the frightening chill that was running up and down his spine, and he slowly walked on, staring intently at the ghostly forms. He heard their low murmur, like the subdued cackle of a witch, and caught a glimpse of ghastly skull-like faces with hollow black eyes. They kept scampering, just beyond the hazy light of the lantern, but then one tripped on the track, and Amos lunged forward to catch it. A fearless, *"bravado"* action, thought the faint-hearted Antonio. Amos caught it by the foot, and the creature bellowed. It was a lamb! There were four of them in the tunnel. They had been living cargo aboard one of the freight trains that crashed weeks earlier and had escaped their pens. A team of men with nets were sent into the tunnel later that day to capture these four-legged ghosts of the Hoosac.

"But what of all the men who died digging this tunnel, surely, there must be a valid haunting concerning them?" I asked, as Felten and I walked back to his truck which was parked at another lot hidden by the weeds. I sat on his runningboard and listened to the history of the making of this miraculous hole through the mountains and the reasons why such a project was attempted in the first place, only a few years after the War of 1812.

Massachusetts farmers and proper Bostonians alike, wanted easy access to upper New York, Pennsylvania and the Mid-West to trade and sell produce and other products. Freight was being hauled by horse wagons or oxen teams at a pace of some two to four miles per hour, and neither could make it over the rugged Hoosac Mountain Range. The Mohawk Indians of New York had earlier blazed a trail over the mountains, which they traversed each summer to invade the Algonquin camps and villages in Massachusetts, but the Indian trail didn't become a passable road until 1843. As early as 1822, it was suggested that locks be built and used to ferry goods over the mountains. But then, the Massachusetts legislature decided that a canal for supply barges be built through the mountains at the base, from the Hoosic River in the West to the Deerfield River in the East. Three years later, the first railroad was built and the canal idea was scraped. Massachusetts put up the money to have the railroad tunnel built through the mountains to gain a route to the West from Boston. It was a Herculean task of hard manual labor started when tunneling was in its infancy. Hundreds of workmen with picks and shovels began pecking away at the base of the mountain, working in two teams, one team digging in from the west and the other from the east, hoping that they would meet somewhere in the middle. Sighting towers were built on the summits, some 1,800 feet above the workmen, so the engineers could determine that everyone was digging in the right direction. Chisels and sledgehammers were also used by the workmen to drill holes in the granite-like rock and then to fill them with black gun-powder. The powder was fused and blasted to break up the rocks, but progress was slower than expected and the blasting was dangerous work. The invention of a huge 75-ton boring machine at Boston in 1851, gave new hope to the project. The machine was towed to Deerfield, where the workmen boasted that the tunnel would be completed within two years. The new boring machine made a 15-inch 24-foot cart-wheel hole in the rock, and then it broke down. No one could ever get the great boring machine started again.

With but a scratch in the mountain, the state legislature gave up the Hoosac Tunnel project for three years. By 1855, some 900 workmen were back with their picks and blackpowder to try again, laboring around the clock each day but Sunday, working in shifts. Into the mountain only twenty feet or more, the sun was blocked out, and the men of all shifts had to carry lanterns so they could see what they were doing. To add further frustration, the men digging on the west side came upon a large conglomerate of various sized boulders called *"puddinstone,"* naturally cemented together, but porous. Gunpowder leaked from the drill holes making blasting impossible. Yet the puddinstones were so hard that picks couldn't crack them. The answer to this new dilemna was power machine drills, run by compressed air, recently introduced to Frenchmen who were successfully digging a tunnel through the Alps. Once this system was introduced at the Hoosac, the workmen could cut into the rock three times faster than by using the old hand-drills and picks. As the west side workers successfully bored through the puddinstone, the eastsiders encountered a new obstacle, which they called, *"porridge-stone."* Inside the mountain, the rock seemed to crumble and break apart easier. But when mixed with the natural springs that flowed into the tunnel from above, it made a thick soupy substance like quicksand which made progress impossible. The porridge-stone problem almost caused the project to be scrapped again. The solution was to hire hundreds of Italian bricklayers to build a roof over the tunnel where the rock crumbled and water poured in. It took months to sop up and stop the flow of porridge with an arched roof seven bricks thick. Over 30 million bricks were used before the drilling workmen could continue their tunneling.

With almost 1,000 men now working at the site in cramped quarters, they were all getting in each others way, impeding progress. To expedite matters, it was decided to dig a shaft from the mountaintop over 1,000 feet down to what would eventually be the middle of the tunnel and set up an elevator system. Thus, diggers could start at the middle and dig east and west to meet the workmen digging towards them from both ends.

The central shaft progressed remarkably well until it reached a depth of 583 feet. A building was constructed at the top of the shaft containing a pump and hoses to keep the flow of springwater out of the shaft, and housing air compressors for power drills and air for the workmen in the shaft. On October 19, 1865, with 13 men digging at the bottom of the shaft, the building at top caught fire. There was no way to extinguish the blaze. Rope was rushed from the town of North Adams and spliced together so that a man could be lowered into the shaft with an airhose in an attempt to save the 13 men in the shaft. A brave volunteer named Tom Mallery was lowered down once the burning embers of the building were cleared away. He was down 40 minutes and then lifted back out, unconscious. When he came to, Mallery reported that the air in the shaft had gone foul. The shaft was filling with water and only burnt timbers were floating on the water. There was no sign of men, dead or alive. It was almost a year later when a new pump and compressor were installed at the top of the shaft and the shaft was pumped out to recover the 13 bodies.

The shaft was reopened and new miners were hired to keep on digging down to the tunnel level at 1,028 feet deep. Then workers, traveling up and down the shaft in an elevator, began digging in opposite directions to meet the two other digging teams from the east and west. Chipped rocks were hauled up the shaft in buckets, and when the center of the tunnel was expanded, mules and carts were lowered into the shaft to carry the rocks to the elevator. The mules lived in the lantern-lit tunnel for four years, without ever seeing daylight.

Besides the 13 who were suffocated in the shaft, nearly 200 men were killed in the tunnel by falling rocks or by rocks piercing them from blasts of gunpowder and glycerine. The most tragic fatality of all, however, was that of miner Tom Lynch. He and his brother, Joe, were blasters working in shifts, tamping and lighting the nitro-glycerine. It was a high-paying job, and a risky occupation. Tom was a bachelor, but Joe was married and had a dozen kids. One afternoon, with Tom's shift about over and Joe soon to replace him, Tom was having a difficult time lighting a glycerine charge which was placed and tamped firmly into the rocks of the tunnel. It was exceptionally damp in the tunnel this day, and as often as he tried, he just couldn't get the fuse to light. If he couldn't do it, his brother would have the responsibility of lighting it on the next shift. The foreman announced the end of the day and the workmen began to leave the tunnel. Tom Lynch insisted he remain behind to light the glycerine before his brother Joe arrived. As the foreman and workers reached daylight at the tunnel entrance, they heard a tremendous explosion. The foreman had warned Tom that the fuse was too short, but Tom didn't want his brother to have the responsibility of lighting it. Tom's funeral was the next day and the casket was closed, for Tom Lynch had blown his own head off.

> "Only a tunneller passing your door, In a solemn hearse to-day; Another bark from life's rough shore launched on the unknown bay."
>
> Tis a risky job to draw a charge of glycerine well tamped in; For the man that tries it, The chances is large that life will be brief for him.
>
> So the cage went up, leaving Tom alone In the shaft, so dreary and dark. A low, deep rumble: 'tis all that's known of the launch of the tunneller's bark."
>
> From a poem by E. A. Wright.

The final blast inside the Hoosac Tunnel, connecting the east and west, was on Thanksgiving Day, November 27, 1873. Besides the workers, there were 600 dignitaries on hand in the center of the tunnel, and they all echoed a cheer, as a five-foot by five-foot hole appeared through the wall of rock, and they all squeezed through to the other side. It had been 24 years of triumph and tragedy, and it cost some seven million dollars to build, yet it takes a train but ten minutes to pass through. After two sets of tracks were layed through the 22 by 24 foot tunnel, the first train steamed through it, coming from Boston and going to New York, on February 9, 1875. Famous poet Oliver Wendell Holmes wrote: *"... When the first locomotive wheels roll through the Hoosac Tunnel bore, Till then let Cummings blaze away, and Miller's saints blow up the globe; But when you see that blessed day, then order your ascension robes."*

For those skeptics like Holmes, the day finally came when the Hoosac became, not only an engineering wonder, but a commercial one as well. But today, only one or two freight-trains pass through each week. Carl Byron, who heads the Hoosac Historical Society, did tell me that the spooky green light that Mr. Felten and I saw inside the tunnel was a signal light for the freight-trains. *"So, then,"* I concluded, *"the tunnel is not haunted."*

"On the contrary," Mr. Byron said, and he told me this story:

"There was an old man who had been the track-walker for some 25 years. He was hired by the railroad to walk the tunnel each day picking rocks that had fallen on the tracks and scaring out any deer or small animals that might have wandered in. In 1975, the old man had a scare himself. His routine all those years had been to start into the tunnel in the morning from the west-end, with his lunch pail in one hand and a lantern in the other. Once he reached daylight at the east portal, he'd sit down on the embankment, eat his lunch and then head back through. This one day, he saw a man carrying a lantern coming towards him at about the center of the tunnel. The track-walker thought little of it, thinking it was probably another railroad worker, but as they passed, the stranger said nothing, not even a greeting came from his lips. Then he noticed from his own light, that the stranger had left no footprints in the dirt and soot where he had just walked. The track-walker turned to look at the back of the man he had just passed in the tunnel. To his horror what he saw was that the stranger had no head!"

A rare photo of a mountain wildcat or bobcat on Mount Willard New Hampshire. They have often been mistaken for cougars and panthers, which are also in the mountains. Photo by Raymond Evans.

VII
CALL Of The WILD

"New England is generally rocky and mountainous," John Josselyn reported to his fellow Englishmen after a fifteen-month visit here in 1638. He also wrote, *"to the Northwest of Scarborow* (Maine), *a ridge of Mountains run Northwest and Northeast a hundred leagues, known by the name of the White Mountains, upon which lieth snow all the year, and is a Landmark twenty miles off at sea."*

Josselyn corrected his error twenty-five years later, returning to New England in 1663 for eight years, during which time he realized that the snow melted even atop Mount Washington during the Summer months. He also did some mountain climbing during his second stay here. Standing atop Sugar Loaf Mountain he said he could *"see the whole country round about,"* and that, *"the country beyond these hills Northward, is daunting terrible, being full of rocky hills as thick as mole-hills in a meadow, and clothed with infinite thick woods."* Even the Indians seemed to avoid this *"terrible"* thick-wooded country. They called it *"Coo-hos,"* meaning *"twisted,"* and the name encompassed all the mountains, hills and valleys from Maine and the Connecticut River up into Canada. Josselyn also complained, whilst in the mountains, *"of black flies, so numerous, that a man cannot draw his breath, but he will suck them in."* Anyone who has visited the mountains of New England in late Spring or early Summer, has experienced the subtle sting and succulent surprise of swallowing the ever swarming little black flies. Like the snow on the mountain peaks, however, they seem to melt away as the Summer progresses.

It seems that Josselyn not only disliked what he saw from the top of Sugar Loaf, but he didn't enjoy the climb either. *"Sugar Loaf,"* he said, *"to outward appearances is a rude heap of massive stones piled one upon another, and you may as you ascend step from one stone to another as if you were going up a pair of stairs. But winding still about the Hill till you come to the top, which will require half a days time and yet is not above a mile."* He did make note during his one day of mountain climbing that he was impressed *"with one stately mountain surmounting the rest,"* meaning Agiocochook, or what we call Mount Washington. *"The Indians shunned the mountain because the great Spirit lived there,"* New Hampshire historian John Anderson tells us in his book about the White Mountains, *"and they called it, Kan Ran Vurgaty, said to be Indian for, the continued likeness of a gull."* The entire mountain range, now known as the Presidential Range, the Indians call *"Waumbek-Methna,"* meaning *"Mounts with snowy fore-*

heads.'' The Indians had given these mountains glorious, meaningful names, yet White Men felt that many of them should be renamed. And this was accomplished with little fanfare, lesser forethought, and no imagination, most of them named after people who have long since been forgotten. *"What a pity that the hills could not have kept the names which the Indian tribes gave them,''* wrote Thomas Starr King, New England's first mountain historian, in 1859. Later, the legislators of New Hampshire thought it fitting to even name a mountain after him.

"The names which the highest peaks of the great range bear were given to them in 1820,'' wrote King, *"by a party from Lancaster. How absurd the order is! Beginning at The Notch, and passing around to Gorham, these are the titles of the summits which are all seen from the village Gorham, Webster, Clinton, Pleasant, Franklin, Monroe, Washington, Clay, Jefferson, Adams, Madison. What a wretched jumble: These are what we have taken in exchange for such Indian words as Agiochook, Ammonoosuc, Moosehillock, Contoocook, Pennacook, Pentucket. Think too, of the absurd association of names which the three mountains that rise over the Franconia Notch are unsuited with—Mount Lafayette, Mount Pleasant and Mount Liberty! How much better to have given the highest peaks of both ranges the names of some great tribes or chiefs, such as Saugus, Passaconaway, Unacanoonuc, Wonnalancent, Weetamoo, Bomazeen, Winnepurkit, Kancamagus—words that chime with Saco, and Merrimack, and Sebago....''*

Mount Washington was appropriately named in 1784, but as Nat Hawthorne wrote after visiting the White Mountains in 1832, *"let us forget the other names of American statesmen that have been stamped upon these hills, but still call the loftiest Washington. Mountains are Earth's undecaying monuments,''* Nat commented after his first climb up Mount Washington. *"They must stand while she endures, and never should be consecrated to the mere great men of their own age and country, but to the mighty ones alone, whose glory is universal, and whom all time will render illustrious.''*

"Even the general name 'White Mountains' is usually inapplicable during the season in which visitors see them,'' wrote Starr King. *"All unwooded summits of tolerable eminence are white in the winter, and in the Summer, the mountains of the Washington range* (Presidential Range), *seen at a distance in the ordinary daylight, are pale, dim green.''* The Green Mountains of Vermont are, of course, white or grey during much of the year, and Maine's Black Mountain Range is hardly ever black, except at night. To add further confusion in attempting to color-code mountains, there are three Black Mountains in New England, one in each of the three northern states. There are also two Blue Mountains, not including the Blue Hills of Massachusetts. It

makes one wonder who were the dumb-clucks that named all these mountains? And who gave them the authority to do so?

The Vermont politicians messed up right from the beginning. Our 14th state was supposed to be named *"New Connecticut,"* but on July 4, 1777, it was agreed that her name be *"Verdmonts,"* meaning *"Green Mountains"* in French. The Congressional delegation apparently started celebrating too early, and the name *"Vermont"* was written into the official name book for eternity, meaning, *"Mountain of Maggots."* In a vain attempt to devulgerize their forefathers' monumental mistake, *"Mountain of Worms,"* is sometimes substituted by Vermonters.

"Verdmont," was the name given to the Green Mountains in October, 1763, by Reverend Peters, the first minister of the mountains. He, with three army colonels named Willis, Taplin and Peters (the Reverend's nephew), climbed to the top of Mount Pisgah with a jug of whiskey and christened the country about them as *"Verdmonts."* A witness to the naming of the territory, Edward Kendall, wrote that Reverend Peters *"harangued the company with a short history of the infant settlement. He then poured the spirits around him, and cast the bottle on the rock.... The ceremony being over, the company descended Mount Pisgah and took refreshments in a log-house, kept by Captain Otley, where they spent the night with great pleasure."*

Timothy Dwight, known as *"Old Pope,"* and President of Yale College in 1795, visited Vermont often. In 1822, he wrote, *"a considerable number of those who first claimed and acquired influences in the state of Vermont during the early periods, were men of loose principles and loose morals. They were either professed infidels, Universalists, or persons who exhibited the morals of these two classes of mankind. We cannot expect, therefore, to find the public measures of Vermont distinguished at that time, by any peculiar proofs of integrity or justice."* If this be true, then maybe naming the state *"Mountain of Maggots,"* wasn't a mistake.

Many Vermont mountainmen were notorious, but some, like Ethan Allen, were famous and genuinely courageous. One of Allen's biographers, Stewart Holbrook, tells us that, one evening while tracking through the mountains, a large catamount, also known as a mountain-lion, leaped onto Ethan's back and tried to eat him alive. *"Reaching up behind its head,"* writes Holbrook, *"Ethan grabbed the big animal around the neck, heaved it forward and to the ground, then strangled it where it lay... When he arrived at Captain Kent's Tavern in Dorset that night, he excused his delay. The damned New Yorkers have trained and set varmints against me,"* he said.

Battling wild animals, Indians, land-grabbing New Yorkers, and British soldiers during the Revolutionary War, Ethan Allen, leader of the *"Green Mountain Boys,"* became a legend in his own time. Even today, this hard drinking, womanizing wild man of the mountains is considered by Vermonters to be their most illustrious son. A multitude of Vermont babies during and after the Revolution were named after this rascally hero. One was Ethan Allen Crawford, son of Vermont's Abel Crawford, who became the pioneering trail-blazer of New Hampshire's White Mountains.

Abel and Ethan cleared the first path to the summit of Mount Washington, and built the first shelter for stranded and exhausted hikers and mountain climbers near the summit. Ethan supplied this hut with emergency equipment, beds and supplies, and carried a heavy eight-foot slab of lead up the mountain on his back, so that those who reached the lofty peaks could scratch their names into it with an iron pencil. He performed this near-herculean task so that mountain visitors wouldn't scratch autographs into the rocks and deface the summit. He was New Hampshire's Paul Bunyan and Johnny Appleseed combined, and like his Vermont namesake, a legend in his own time. Nat Hawthorne, visiting the Crawford House Inn in 1832, writes: *"Among several persons collected about the doorsteps, the most remarkable was a sturdy mountaineer of six-feet-two and corresponding bulk, with a heavy set of features, such as might be moulded on his own blacksmith's anvil, yet indicative of mother wit and rough humor."* This was Ethan Allen Crawford. *"As we appeared, he uplifted a tin trumpet, four or five feet long, and blew a temendous blast, either in honor of our arrival or to awaken an echo from the opposite hill."*

Ethan Allen Crawford was with the mountain climbing party Starr King complained about, when they trekked up Mount Washington in 1820, and gave the mountains their patriotic names. Ethan, however, was only the guide, and he wasn't allowed to join the others in naming the mountains. Yet, if anyone had the right to rename these mountains, it was Ethan Allen Crawford.

Among the group who had taken the day off from busy schedules to rename these natural monuments of New Hampshire (which the Indians had properly named hundreds of years before) were Amos Legro, a surveyor, Adinio Bracket, a map-maker, John Weeks, a soldier, Charles Stewart, a lawyer, and Philip Carrigan, New Hampshire's Secretary of State, who later had a mountain named for him. Within minutes, scanning the horizon and pointing to each mountain within sight, they pealed off the names from second highest peak to lowest, *"Adams, Jefferson, Madison, Monroe,"* then, deciding that maybe all the mountains shouldn't be named after presidents, they dubbed the next one *"Franklin,"* we suppose, after Ben. Their dastardly eternal deed completed, they broke open a bottle of whiskey, and christened each mountain with a swallow. Then they shot off fireworks, drank some more of the whiskey, mixed with Lake of the Clouds water, and stumbled back down to Lancaster. They probably should have decided on names for the mountains after they had consumed the bottle of whiskey, with the slight possibility that they might have then been inspired to come up with creative names like the Indians had before them.

Adding insult to injury, when French General Lafayette visited New England four years later, the dominant mountain of the Franconia Range, then called *"Great Haystack,"* was renamed Mount Lafayette. *"Little Haystack"* was renamed for President Garfield when he was assasinated. Fortunately, the fad of renaming New England's mountains after live dignitaries and dead presidents has also died out. But only a few precious Indian names remain—all having a majestic ring to them: *"Wachusett, Moosilauke, Woumbek, Passaconaway, Monadnock,"* and my favorite, *"Katahdin."* Maine's loftiest peak.

Katahdin, so the Indians believed, was the birthplace of all storms. Living at the summit was their spirit-god, *"Pamoola,"* who could brew up a thunderstorm, blizzard, or hurricane, at a moments notice. No one knows what a real thunderstorm is until they've experienced one at Mount Katahdin. The surrounding countryside of Aroostock County, Maine, is not only known as the Potato Frontier, but as *"the land of lightning."* In July and August of each year, the flashes and din from the peaks of Katahdin leave no one questioning the power of *Pamoola.*

There are many who visit Katahdin, like the Indians of old, who believe that *Pamoola* is not just a spirit, but is real flesh and blood. The Indians considered it a living devil of enormous strength that would kill animals and Indians, but not White Men. In 1866, a Maine mountaineer named Cluey, reported that he saw *Pamoola* while he was panning for gold on Katahdin. *"It was on the banks of a pond that I saw it on the opposite bank,"* said Cluey, who was a noted mountain guide. *"It was eating raw fish alive. It was man-like, but covered with red hair, and stood almost seven-feet tall. It was there at Twilight and again at Dawn, but it didn't see me."* The red-headed *Pamoola* has also been seen from time to time, as late as 1987, in and around Topsfield, Maine, and is known there as the *"Indian Devil."* A group of Massachusetts boy scouts met up with *Pamoola* on a camping trip to Katahdin in September of 1988. They saw it from a distance at the edge of the woods, *"grubbing the wood-roots for food,"* said one boy scout. *"It stunk like rotten eggs,"'* commented another frightened boy, *"even though we weren't that close to it."* Even after it had run off, other campers who had come onto the scene and had seen the creature as well, reported, *"the smell remained in the area, hours after it had run off."* The boy scout leader, who wished to remain anonymous, said that, *"it had a triangular face, reddish-brown fur, and made a series of frightening sounds—Needless to say, the boys and I didn't camp out on the mountain that night."* Six other out-of-state mountain climbers also saw the Bigfoot-like creature that same day on Mount Katahdin.

"A Wildman Of The Mountains Scares Two Young Vermont Hunters," was a front-page headline of the New York Times, on October 18, 1879. Although the article does not give the names of the hunters, the *"Wildman"* sounds like *Pamoola,* or at least a smaller close relative. The story read as follows: *"The young men described the creature as being about five feet high, resembling a man in form and movement, but colored all over with bright red hair and having a long straggling beard, and with very wild eyes. When first seen the creature sprang from behind a rocky cliff, and started for the woods nearby, when, mistaking it for a bear, one of the men fired, and, it is thought, wounded it, for with fierce cries of pain and rage, it turned on its assailants, driving them before it at high speed. They lost their guns and ammunition in their flight and dared not return for fear of encountering the strange being."* This ocurred in the mountains near the Vermont border at Williamstown, Massachusetts. Could this wild creature be a Bigfoot, or a Yeti, which seem to be so prevalent on the Northwest Coast of our country? Or are these encounters with hairy beings merely chance meetings with men gone wild?

Men have, throughout history, wandered into the mountains to live lives of quiet desperation alone, avoiding all contact with other humans. Or they could have been lost in the mountains during a hunting or climbing trip, driven themselves into insanity and continued to wander the mountains, afraid when they met up unexpectedly with other humans. Paul Doherty, who tracks lost hunters for the New Hampshire Fish and Game Department, says that most lost people are frightened, do strange things, and are almost in a state of panic when he finds them. *"Many run and hide on me when I spot them,"* says Paul.

In January, 1984, two distraught Vietnam veterans had voluntarily wandered up into the Berkshire Mountains near Greenfield, Massachusetts, in an attempt to live out the remainder of their nightmarish lives without contact with other humans. Unfortunately, they came upon a Buddhist Shrine in the mountains, which they set on fire. It in turn igniting the surrounding woods, along with their pent-up rage, and this prompted police to track them down and bring them back to civilization. *"There are at least three more*

Vietnam veterans living off the land in the state's Western mountains," reported Brian Willson, Director of the Massachusetts Vietnam Veterans of America, *"and many more living in seclusion in the mountains of New Hampshire, Vermont and Maine."*

One of the strangest stories of a child lost in the mountains, occurred at Alstead, New Hampshire near the Vermont border, in 1770. It is told by Seth Arnold, the Congregational Minister of Alstead: *"The child was three year old Jacob Cady, lost from his grandmother Hodskin's house, upon the hill at East Alstead. Jacob's Dad, Issac, was choppin wood by the barn, and Jacob begged his Ma in the cabin to let him outside to help chop wood. She let him leave the house, but a half-hour later, when Issac came in the house, he told his wife that he hadn't even seen little Jacob. They went outside and called him, but there was no answer. Members of the family then searched the property, fields, woods, and then asked neighbors to join them in their search. When night set in, over 400 men and women carrying torches, combed the nearby woods and hills. Residents from other nearby villages and towns joined in the search, and continued, many of them without sleep, for two more days and nights. On the eve of the third day, when there was little hope of finding the three year old alive, he was discovered alive in a mountain cave, two miles from his grandmother's house. He was hiding from his rescuers, for he said that he thought they were wild Indians, but he told his rescuers that he received food and drink which kept him alive, 'from a nice big black dog. I suckled milk from it too,' he told them. When Jacob grew to be a strong young man, he said that he still remembered the black dog, but I fear that, he then realized, it was probably a wolf."*

Henry David Thoreau, New England's illustrious naturalist, one day in 1860, invited his poet friend Ellery Channing to camp out for a week with him on New Hampshire's Mount Monadnock. Channing, who had never climbed a mountain, nor camped on one, reluctantly agreed. Thoreau later wrote that Channing *"was ready to decamp after a couple of days, and it was only after several nights,"* he revealed, *"that Channing realized he was lying out-doors."* Channing's only inquiry of Thoreau during their mountain venture was, *"what is the largest creature that might nibble my legs up here?"*

Although Channing didn't return to the mountains for some thirteen years after his campout with Thoreau, he later overcame his fears, became an avid mountain climber, and was author of the popular *"Monadnock Journal."* But to answer his initial question of Thoreau, there are bears, wolves, cougars and panthers that might *"nibble your legs"* while in the New England mountains! Bobcats and lynx, although rare, also can be found in the mountains and have been mistaken for cougars. But lynx and bobcat are usually only three-feet long, whereas a cougar or panther can measure nine-feet and weigh over 200 pounds. It was thought by many hunters that the last New England cougar was killed in the Green Mountains in 1881—it was seven-feet long and weighed 183 pounds. More have been seen in the mountains since then.

In the Berkshire Mountains of Massachusetts, a creature Pittsfield folks call, *"The Thing,"* periodically rears its ugly head, frightening tourists and hikers. It is a large black cat, approximately eight-feet long, and not only has it been seen from time to time, but its horrific screech, like that of a hysterical woman in distress, echoes through the hills above Pittsfield, sending chills up and down the spines of residents and visitors alike. A similar creature in size and color has been seen in the mountains near Wilton, New Hampshire. One man who spotted it was Charles Proctor, the State Conservation Officer. He believes the creature lives on Temple Mountain. Gore Mountain, Vermont also contains a large cougar, reddish-brown in color, which has been seen and identified by state officials and a qualified naturalist. A few years ago, two fawn colored cougars were spotted and chased by Sheriff's deputies near Dalton, New Hampshire. The pair were tracked into the mountains by hunters and hounds from Bedell's Farm. The dogs were attacked by the cats and the hounds retreated, as did the Sheriff and his men. There was a similar incident recently near Springfield, Vermont, when local hunter Kirk Heath and his dogs tracked a pair of large black panthers for two days through the snow. During the chase, the panthers took time out to kill four deer, but ate only their lungs and liver and then moved on. *"My dogs closed in on them a few times,"* Kirk reported to the local paper, *"but the cats escaped into the mountains."* In August of 1988, Doris Cox, visiting Mount Katahdin, Maine on a fishing trip with her husband, was pursued into her cabin by a frisky black panther, some ten-feet long. It kept her confined for almost half a day, standing sentinel outside the cabin door, while her husband William was peacefully fishing in a pond a few miles away. *"The panther,"* says Doris, *"apparently got bored stalking me and wandered back into the woods."* Maine loggers also report sighting panthers on the highway, usually at Twilight, in the sparsely settled northern part of the state.

Obviously, the last cougar or panther of New England wasn't killed, as reported, in 1881. Nor was the last New England wolf shot in 1968 on the Vermont-New Hampshire border, as was officially reported by police and press. Along the Canadian border at Vermont, New Hampshire and Maine, there were hundreds of reports in the late 1960's and early 1970's of domestic dogs and farm animals being found dead, obviously attacked by wild animals, but with only their hearts eaten out. This caused some of the superstitious mountain folks to think there was a vampire in their midst. At night, however, they could hear the mournful howls and realized that wolves had returned to their mountains. Maine Fish and Game officials managed to shoot two of these six-foot long wolf-like creatures, weighing about 45 pounds each, in 1975, and the carcasses were shipped to the Biology Department of Harvard College for analysis. Harvard concluded that these predators of the Northland that attacked like timber-wolves just for the sport of it, yet looked like German Shepherds, were neither wolf nor dog, but a combination of both. A new animal, they originated as coyotes from the West Coast of America, and traveling East through Southern Canada, bred with wolves and possibly domestic dogs gone wild. By the time this new breed reached northern New England about 25 years ago, they began procreating like rabbits and killing every wild and domestic animal that crossed their path. They are known today as *"coydogs,"* and traveling in packs are extremely dangerous. They are as fierce as timber-wolves, sly as foxes, resistant as coyotes, and more intelligent than German Shepherds. There are now an estimated 40,000 coydogs in New England, their population seemingly concentrated around Conway, New Hampshire and Dexter, Maine. Maine hunters and trappers have already killed over 300 coydogs in and around Dexter over the past few years. Trapper Horace Farrar of Dexter, ships in coyote urine from Wyoming, which he uses to bait his traps. *"When the coydogs come around my traps,"* says Horace, *"the urine makes them think that a coyote has been in the area, and they believe it's safe to travel on, and that's how I trap them."* Coydogs in packs are adept at killing sheep, cows, horses and deer. There are no reports of them attacking humans, yet.

There is, therefore, little doubt that wild dogs, wild cats, and wild men roam the mountains of New England. But even wilder than these is the constant changing weather of the highlands, and the howling winds of Mount Washington. They are the strongest winds ever recorded anywhere in the world. As Ethan Allen Crawford said in 1823, *"the wind comes down the narrows of the Notch from the mountains with such violence that it requires two men to hold one man's hair on."* A Captain Parker of Boston, who was forced to retreat to Crawford's shelter on Mount Washington in 1825, told Ethan, *"I have experienced gales in the Gulf Stream, tempests off Cape Hatteras, tornadoes in the West Indies, and have been surrounded by waterspouts in the Gulf of Mexico, but I never saw anything more furious or more dreadful than this wind."*

Mount Washington is not only the highest point in New England, 6,288 feet above sea level, but is one of the coldest spots in America, with the temperature dropping to minus 50 degrees fahrenheit or lower in the winter, and below freezing in the summer. Ice can form at the summit at any time during the year, and it often snows there in June and September. The highest wind velocity ever recorded on earth, on April 12, 1934, was 231 mile-per-hour at the summit of Mount Washington, and winds gusting up to 250 miles an hour have been unofficially recorded. Steady 100 mile-per-hour winds are frequent. It was here that the United States Army tested all foul-weather gear during World War II, because those were the worst weather conditions that the American military could find anywhere in the world. Where else can you experience hurricane-force winds and sub-Arctic temperatures for almost half the year, while some six-thousand feet below, people are swimming and sunbathing?

"To be fastened one night on Mount Washington alone," wrote Starr King in 1876, *"I am sure would almost crush my reason."* When he did spend one night atop Mount Washington with others in the Summit House, he reported his nightmarish experience by saying, *"as I lay under the blankets, that view of the sky haunted me and drove away sleep. And other terrors connected with darkness and the storm on Mount Washington, were present also."* One may wonder what these *"other terrors"* are that Starr King mentions, but those who know the mountain realize he is talking about the ever-present mysterious monster of Mount Washington, called *"The Presence."*

Almost everyone who spends a night on Mount Washington has felt *"The Presence"* in one way or another. It is a powerful ghostly spirit that haunts the summit. *"It is not an evil force, just mischievous,"* says Lee Vincent, one of the directors who lives and works at the Observation and Transmitter Station atop the mountain. *"It plays with us up here on the mountain,"* said Peter Zwirken of the weather observatory. *"It seems to pick on people it doesn't like and then forces them off the mountain."* Another observatory worker, Mike Micucci, swears that while walking along a platform outside the transmitter hut, *"the Presence tried to push me off the mountain, and I've got bruises on my arm to prove it."*

"On one blustery evening," said Zwirken, *"with all of us inside the huts, there came a knock at the door. When we opened it to one of our typical snowy, stormy nights, there, sitting on our doorstoop was a large, heavy bronze plaque. We recognized it as a familiar memorial to a mountain climber who had died of exposure on the mountain. The plaque came from a stone foundation at Crawford Path a mile away. It had been ripped off its foundation and somehow transported to our door atop Mount Washington— No mortal could have accomplished such a feat."* Peter also admits that, *"a person really can't spend too many days and nights up there at a time."*

Zwirken himself suffered a serious fall on the mountain, and was forced to leave work for an extended period. *"Living up here can set a guy's nerves on end,"* Bill Harris, a television engineer, agrees, *"and I do feel 'the Presence' up here from time to time, and when I do, I know it's time to take a break down the mountain."* The mountaintop workers hear voices and footsteps, yet no one is there to produce them, and articles move or are suspended in mid-air inside the buildings—it is an ever present, yet illusive, unseen creature.

Greg Gordon, who worked many years on Mount Washington, believes that the savage winds and harsh weather conditions cause these strange sensations. *"The wind wails like a freight-train, and you feel like you're on another planet,"* says Greg. *"Even inside the buildings and huts, they shake and rattle constantly, and the interior of the buildings can become a vacuum. Opening the front door of the observatory,"* Gordon explained, *"never failed to trigger a rather elaborate sequence of events—a loud hissing would precede the opening of the cellar door, which would then bang violently into the clothes-rack. All of the clothes would then extend themselves horizontally in the direction of the hallway, the trap-door in the kitchen would rise and fall a foot, and then came clattering back down in place. When the terrific suction would at last slam the front door shut, one's ears would pop...."*

Whether real or imagined, there are certainly strange forces at work atop Mount Washington. The Indians, as our first historians tell us, feared the mountain, and would not venture to its summit, and their ancient name for the mountain, *Agiocochook,* means *"Home of the Great Spirit."* Probably, that powerful prankish ghost called *"The Presence,"* by White Men, and *"The Great Spirit,"* by Indians, is one and the same, and it broods above the tree-line of the mountain, awaiting a visit from lowlanders such as you and me, so that it might gleefully pounce on us.

Those who are new to the mountains, or are visiting them for the first time, are called *"goofers"* by the more experienced mountaineers, and it's not just the mischievous *"Presence"* that enjoys dealing with *"goofers"* during their first night in the mountains. There are thousands of new hikers, campers, skiers, climbers, and just plain nature lovers, who visit these mountains each year. In Ethan Allen Crawford's White Mountains, the Appalachian Mountain Club provides food, shelter and conviviality throughout the mountain chain with a series of rustic huts, run by a group of young men and women called *"hutsters."* The *hutsters* and their hostels are a welcome respite for anyone attempting to hike these rugged mountains. Without them, many who challenge the mountains would never return to the peaceful valleys below yet, even with them there, ready for every conceivable emergency, an average of two people lose their lives in the White Mountains every year, and have since 1888, the year the first stone hut was built in the mountains at Madison Spring. The *hutsters*, among their many varied duties, must lug materials and food supplies up the mountain on their backs almost every day. In many instances, this is a three-mile near vertical climb, sometimes with up to 100 pounds tied to a backpack. Three teenaged *hutsters* once packed a Model A Ford pick-up truck, section by section, excluding the motor, up to Madison Hut, an altitude of 4,825 feet. It took them almost the entire summer, but they finally reassembled the truck outside the hut. It remains a puzzle to *"goofers,"* who can't imagine how the truck made the impossible drive up the steep side of the mountain.

These nine mountain lodges, or huts as they are called, are spaced throughout the mountain range so that a truly active *goofer* can travel along the 56-mile crest of the mountains for eight days, spending each night in a different hut. One of the typical pranks on *goofers* is for the *hutsters* to switch hut-crews during the middle of the night, so that when the *goofers* hike on to the next hut, arriving thoroughly exhausted, they will find the same smiling *hutsters* awaiting them. The *hutsters* also enjoy putting out lobster-traps each morning in the nearby fresh water ponds and streams, amazing out-of-state *goofers* when the traps filled with lobsters, are pulled in the evening, which are eaten for dinner with great relish. Alan Corindia, once a *hutster*, now Director of the Applachian Mountain Club, recently said, *"Surely many goofers from places like Colorado or Utah, go back home to tell friends about the lobster they ate that was trapped from the ponds of the White Mountains, never realizing that they had been the victims of a put-on."*

From the biggest hut, *"Lakes of the Clouds"* at Mount Washington, which accomodates 90 guests, to the smallest *"Zealand Falls Hut,"* which can house 36 overnight guests, the entertainment on those stormy, windy nights is the telling of ghost stories. The favorite subjects are, of course, Pamoola and the *Presence*. Before the night is over, at least one panther, wolf, or cougar comes scratching at the door. Yet, when all is said and done, probably the only thing one has to fear in the mountains is the *hutsters* and their inevitable practical jokes. Like the wild winds and those wondrous views, the *hutsters* have that unique ability of leaving you breathless, but they also provide some of that magic that can be found only in the mountains of New England.